MURRAY WALKER

The _{very} last word

D0233866

Other books by this author:

Murray Walker
The last word (hardback)

Michael Schumacher
The greatest of all?

Inside the mind of the Grand Prix driver
The psychology of the fastest men on earth: sex,danger,
and everything else

Michael Schumacher
The Ferrari years

The motorsport art of Juan Carlos Ferrigno

Hitler's Grands Prix in England
Donington 1937 and 1938

Ayrton Senna
As time goes by

Ayrton Senna
The legend grows

Ayrton Senna
His full car racing record

MURRAY WALKER

The ^very last word

CHRISTOPHER HILTON

Haynes Publishing

First edition (hardback) published in October 2001 as
Murray Walker – The last word
Second edition (paperback) published in August 2002, with additional text, as *Murray Walker – The very last word*

A catalogue record for this book is available from the British Library

ISBN 1 85960 895 7

Library of Congress control no 2002 107 493

Haynes North America Inc., 861 Lawrence Drive, Newbury Park, California 91320, USA.

Published by Haynes Publishing, Sparkford, Nr Yeovil, Somerset BA22 7JJ, UK.
Tel: 01963 442030 Fax: 01963 440001
Int.tel: +44 1963 442030 Int.fax: +44 1963 440001
E-mail: sales@haynes-manuals.co.uk
Website: www.haynes.co.uk

Designed and typeset by Glad Stockdale, Sutton
Printed and bound in Britain by J. H. Haynes & Co. Ltd, Sparkford

CONTENTS

The years never touched the enthusiasm.

INTRODUCTION

When the talking finally stopped – the official talking, anyway – something astonishing happened.

That night at the Theatre Royal in Drury Lane, London, the personalities of showbusiness paraded themselves for the 2002 British Academy Television Awards. Some of the starlets wore very little and other starlets wore less than that. Once the cameras had stopped feasting on them and panned across the audience, you could pick out a couple of dozen celebrated actors and actresses – people who knew their way around Shakespeare as well as soap operas.

George Best came onto the stage to make the presentation for sport. The candidates were the 'British Grand Prix 2001 – farewell to Murray Walker', the FA Cup Final, Channel 4 cricket and the Germany versus England soccer match. The soccer got it.

Much later the dapper figure of Sir Jackie Stewart appeared on the stage and said 'British motorsport has been a great success for our country and the man who has been part of that success tonight receives a special award. He has excited radio listeners and television audiences all around the world in a frenzy of enthusiasm. His voice is instantly recognised by millions. His integrity is above reproach even if occasionally some of his facts are ... questionable.'

That was greeted by a rumbling murmur of appreciation which broadened into gales of laughter. They knew, although no name had been mentioned. A compilation of film clips was shown on a big screen, beginning inevitably with 'One ... two ... three ... four .... five lights. GO! GO! GO!' The clips included archive footage of a young Murray Walker, the breathless finish to the 1969 Italian Grand Prix, Damon Hill's 1996 World Championship in Japan (both these races are in Chapter 11) and one of my particular favourites: a BMW accelerated along a wet country circuit and Walker was assuring viewers that the driver 'looks through a completely clean windscreen. That's the big advantage, of course, of being in front' – and as he spoke those fateful words the car plunged off and battered itself against a grassy bank.

The Theatre Royal exploded with mirth.

He sat with his wife Elizabeth, and Stewart – in his lilting Scottish accent – said 'a remarkable man that we all love very deeply. Murray McWalker!' The applause was like rolling thunder. It followed Murray all the way up on to the stage. He said 'I feel I've made it at last! I never, ever, in a million years dreamed that I would be up here receiving an award like this. It's 52 years since I did my first British Grand Prix at Silverstone ... I've had a fabulous life and if you've enjoyed it you haven't enjoyed it half as much as I have. So thank you very much everyone.' The thunderous applause rolled again.

A funny peculiar thing. I first interviewed him in 1982, when he had *already* been doing race commentaries for 30 years, and I had no idea what he looked like. Neither, he assured me, did anybody else. The BBC hardly ever showed him, although when he got into taxis and spoke, the drivers recognised him immediately. Twenty years further on – as the BAFTA award demonstrated so vividly – he had become one of the most recognisable people in the country, and in Australia, and New Zealand, and Canada, and South Africa.

The serious aspect is that, in the transition from being just a voice to a genuine cult figure, Murray Walker did not change at all. The man who took the stage to receive the 2002 award was exactly the man who greeted me in his Hertfordshire home all those years before. He was courteous, perceptive, with a laugh vibrating with enthusiasm, wise in the ways of the world. Here was a man with a surprising life story: serving as a tank commander during the War, selling aspirins in the Indian subcontinent, becoming a powerful advertising executive.

The reason I'd wanted to interview him in 1982 was simple. His commentaries were known for their too supercharged delivery (he insisted the BBC had asked him to reduce the decibel level a bit) and he was known for mistakes. But he was philosophical about these even then. He had reached an acceptance with himself that if you are to commentate live on something as fast, unpredictable and spread out as a motor race, you cannot avoid the mistakes. Of course neither he nor I could have remotely imagined that in the fullness of time these mistakes would become celebrated in their own right and adorn banners, Internet websites and tee shirts.

He says himself that 'a very, very large part of what success I've had, in my opinion, is due to the fact that I happen to have a voice that suits my sport. I am dealing with a harsh, aggressive, fast-moving sport and I have a harsh, aggressive, fast-moving voice.'

By the time of his final Grand Prix commentary – in the United States in 2001 – he was 78 going on 18. His enthusiasm seemed to be growing and the decibel level was still a formidable challenge for your neighbours on a quiet Sunday afternoon.

To find a commentator to replace Murray Walker was by definition always going to be extremely difficult, if not impossible. Tony Jardine, an integral part of the ITV coverage, says 'we all still very much miss him but we know that he is never coming back full time. We're in a post-Murray era – where we've got to all play to our strengths. You can't replace a unique guy like that, you have to do it through team-work and that's what we're trying to do.'

Murray was not lost altogether. He continued to contribute to ITV on an occasional basis and described the races for the Orange mobile phone company. Debbie Wall of Orange explains that 'we have a system where you can ring in and get updates on all sorts of things, from where to go out partying in London, through to sport. We wanted to use Murray to do something in Formula 1 – it was natural for us, because it's all about voice rather than anything else. So we approached him to see if he'd be interested in doing a race update for our 277 service after each Grand Prix. If you dial 277 on your mobile you get given a load of options: sport, news and entertainment. F1 or whatever. Murray is within the F1 part.

'On a Sunday night he gets on the phone, dials into an automated system and records his three-minute synopsis of the race weekend. That can be anything from who's going to sign for who, to what happened on the track. Mainly it's track activity but he'll give you a bit of gossip, too, while he goes through it. Can he do exactly three minutes? Oh yes.'

Don't be misled by how affable and approachable he is. Don't let the beautiful blunders distort your view. Murray Walker was a gentleman and a consummate professional. Let's GO! GO! GO! right back to the beginning and follow his career all the way through.

'At this point the colonel recommended that I be demoted to the rank of corporal.'

1

SON OF THE FATHER

Murray Walker was born in Birmingham, an only child, to Graham and Elsie. There are no reports of how fast the delivery was. He was born into motor racing because that was what Graham, a First World War dispatch rider, did. Graham rode competitively between 1920 and 1935. Elsie (*née* Spratt) was 'the daughter of what used to be called a draper,' Murray says. 'She was an extremely strong-minded woman who was born and brought up in Leighton Buzzard in Bedfordshire. My father was injured by a shell in France during World War One and part of his recuperation involved him being in Leighton Buzzard. He met my mother there and set his cap at her, as they say. They married in 1922, I was produced in 1923.'

For the first 12 years of his life young Murray travelled Europe to races with Graham. The centrepiece of that world was the Isle of Man, where the Tourist

Trophy races were held every summer. Murray once said it became so normal that he couldn't understand little boys who *didn't* go. He has also related that his mother scolded him because, at the age of five, he sat in the grandstand reading his comics, oblivious to the great deeds unfolding before him. However, 'to be brutally honest I used to enjoy being the son of Graham Walker because he was big-time and wherever he went people used to make a fuss of him. Therefore people made a fuss of me and my mother.'

Although the family lived in Enfield he became a boarder at a North London school (Highgate, where his father had gone) and initially wasn't particularly drawn to motorsport. It was just what dad did, and what dad continued to do after his retirement from racing. Graham edited a magazine called *Motor Cycling* and commentated. Only later, perhaps, did Murray understand the profound influence his father had had on him. Murray holds his memory in the utmost respect as well as affection – although he did tell me Graham was such a heavy smoker 'he needed a cigarette to get him over to the mantelpiece to get his pipe!'

' *And the first five places are filled by five different cars* '

Murray would remember that Graham 'conceived the idea of having a thing called Donington Day and *Motor Cycling* invited all their readers to come to

Donington and all the manufacturers came. It was obligatory that any manufacturer's representative should ride to the meeting on a motor cycle of his own firm's manufacture. It was an absolutely fabulous day.'

In 1937 Murray went to the car Grand Prix at Donington, an almost hypnotic event because the mighty Mercedes and Auto Union cars were there. A well-known South African cartoonist was a family friend and 'he drove my mother and I to Donington in a BSA Scout, which was a front-wheel-drive so-called sports car. There was room for one person to sit sideways in the back – guess who sat sideways in the back? I had an absolutely fabulous time because that was the first time the Auto Unions came here and we had another family friend, Joe Woodhouse, who had made a lot of money in Germany and retired. He was interpreter for the Auto Union and Mercedes-Benz teams when they came to English-speaking events.

'I was very lucky because I came up as part of the Mercedes-Benz entourage. I was a starry-eyed enthusiast about motor racing, and still am. I stood next to Major General Huhnlein who was the boss of motorsport in Germany. I stood next to Bernd Rosemeyer, Hermann Lang, Rudolf Caracciola – I've got all their autographs at home.'

The next year the Germans were back and so was Murray, impressed by the very serious way they approached motor racing (at that time, the British drivers were gallant chaps in tiny sit-up-and-beg cars).

He remembers 'the publicity material by the Germans, who were gigantically switched on and they handed you all sorts of photographs. You know people do brass rubbings in churches – well, they gave you papier mâché that you could put a piece of paper over and rub with a pencil and you got these beautiful pictures of the drivers and the cars. They had badges and brochures – things which did not exist in our world. Tazio Nuvolari had his little gold tortoise [a lucky mascot, worn round his neck] and Auto Union produced a limited run of those.' Most of all, Walker remembers, 'I stood next to my all-time hero Nuvolari just before he got in the car to win in 1938.'

'*And there's a dry line appearing in the tunnel*'

By now he had begun racing motorcycles at places like Cadwell Park and Brands Hatch, 'which was then anti-clockwise and hadn't even got tarmac on.'

War was coming and in September 1939 Walker found himself in Austria. 'My father was running the British Army team in the international six-days motorcycle trial.' Austria had been incorporated into Greater Germany and 'the team had gone out in the expectation of there being a war and the War Office had promised to send a telegram in the event of things being so dire that we all needed to get back immediately.' The telegram arrived but after a delay of 24 hours. The conclusion was that the team and the Walkers should have beaten a hasty retreat *yesterday*. They prepared to beat a hasty retreat *now*. 'There was the question of whether to go to Switzerland – which you could reach quicker, but you faced possible internment – or take a chance and dash to France. And that's what we did.'

They reached home just in time to hear on their wireless Neville Chamberlain announcing that Britain was now at war with Germany.

When Murray left school (mathematics hampered him from getting what was then known as Matriculation) he joined Dunlop *and* volunteered for the forces. 'I wanted to go into tanks. Don't ask me why I wanted to go into tanks. I expect I wanted a glamorous job to the extent that you could have one in the war. There was no question of my flying an aeroplane, because of the glasses, and there was no question of me being in a submarine because I didn't actually think of that, let alone fancy it.' What the 19-year-old had was a 'mental concept of me with my head sticking out of a tank turret, banners flying – at the time when we were storming across the Western desert, blowing Rommel away. Anyway, if you waited for conscription you got sent to where they wanted you to go – maybe the Pioneer Corps operating smoke canisters in Wolverhampton. I volunteered for tanks.'

Meanwhile 'I got a business scholarship at Dunlop and I went to Birmingham, and it was a bloody, bloody good thing. They put you through every aspect of the business – production, design, engineering, accountancy, the law, marketing, distribution – and you had the best people in the company teaching you or people who were employed from outside as experts to do it. I did that as part time until my call came, then I was in the Army for over four years.'

After a spell at the tank training centre at Bovington, in Dorset, he did the War Office Selection Board, 'a hoop you had to jump through so they could decide if you were officer material.' This included mental agility tests (he *must* have done well) and what he'd describe as sliding down ropes over rivers. 'Then I went to Sandhurst, did my time there and became an officer. I decided I wanted to go to the Royal Scots Greys, which was an extremely coffee-in-the-lounge cavalry regiment – the last cavalry regiment in the British army to be mechanised.' He fought for 'the rest of the war – Holland, and across Germany. I was involved in the crossing of the Rhine, which was a bloody unpleasant thing. We did the link-up with the Russians. I was a lieutenant at this time.'

With Germany disintegrating, the British, Americans and Canadians were pouring east and 'the Germans were coming westwards as fast as they could to get away from the Russians. At one point, I vividly remember, we were going up a road, a sort of country lane, in a column of British tanks and the German army – in trucks, jeeps, motorbikes and cars – were coming down the same piece of road in the opposite direction. These were the chaps we'd been taught to hate, despise, kill. You'd stop. There'd be a staff car full of German officers, us in our tanks, each stolidly ignoring the other.'

Typically he'd recount a story against himself (and I'm indebted to Tony Jardine for passing it on). He was up in the turret with a map and binoculars – the whole thing – leading a tank convoy which rumbled along behind him. 'Come on!' he said and led it up a dead end. The road was so narrow that the convoy couldn't turn round and had to reverse.

'WALKER!'

'Yes, sir?'

Many years later, Roger Moody – who produced the BBC's *Grand Prix* programme – formed the impression that Murray 'had a very colourful life in the Army and he used to regale us with some of those tales. He wasn't a saint in those days, he enjoyed himself. Incidentally, I'm sure the training he had as a young man there, as well as literally following in his father's footsteps, has stood him in good stead all his working life.'

(Many years later too he took part in an Easter television programme based around motorsport and celebrities. Barry Sheene, for example, was paired with pop singer Roger Daltry. Murray was given a tank to drive and evidently took it off downhill, much to the consternation of those watching. He knew what he was doing, of course.)

Murray's military service ended at a passing out parade in front of Field Marshal Montgomery, an almost mythical figure who had commanded the Eighth Army in North Africa, but before then Murray had been given special leave to go to the 1946 Manx Grand Prix. It wasn't quite that simple though. He had been made 'technical adjutant of the regiment, which is in charge of all the mechanical aspects of a mechanised regiment, and I was 21 years old so it was, if I say so myself, no mean achievement. It carried the more substantive rank of captain and the colonel wouldn't give me the rank, basically because I was a Johnny-come-lately wartime soldier, not a peacetime soldier, and it was a very, very regular regiment. I had a gigantic bust-up with him, as a result of which he filed a very adverse report on me: being drunk in the mess, fraternising with German women – both of which were true, but not every officer got reported for it – and a string of other things.' The colonel cancelled his leave to go to the Manx Grand Prix but a brigadier, called in to adjudicate, came down on Walker's side.

'At this point the colonel had recommended that I be demoted to the rank of corporal, and I was a captain. When the brigadier made that judgement, there was no man on earth whom the colonel hated more than Murray Walker. So the brigadier said "no way can you stay in the regiment ... you are now appointed as technical adjutant of the British Army of the Rhine Armoured Fighting Vehicles Schools at Belsen, the concentration camp, with the rank of captain."' The camp, however, had been cleaned up by then.

He had seen action and known fear but, overall, he'd enjoyed the Army.

'I'm not a natural wheeler-dealer or anything like that. I just thought I'll go back to Dunlop, they'll have me ... and they did have me, so when I started racing bikes I was working for Dunlop – which is what I had always wanted to do, work in advertising.' He also wanted to be a rider and competed in 'trials and that sort of thing' but wasn't really good enough and he knew it. He'd stay close to motorsport, though, through his father – and by chance.

'Senna 1st, Prost 2nd and Berger 3rd – that makes the top four'

In competitive terms, as he's said, he wanted to be a Stirling Moss and half a century later I relayed that to Moss, now Sir Stirling. 'Oh really!' he said. I wondered if Moss ever wanted to be Murray Walker? 'No, but I have the greatest respect for him.' But his career has gone on to the age of 78. 'Well, I'm hoping mine will, too, so shut up.' In June 2001 Moss competed in the historic race at Le Mans. He is six years younger than Murray.

It is important to emphasise the point that Murray was, and is, much more than a commentator. He recounted to me how, after the war, he happened upon a highly unorthodox and adventurous way of making money. He went to India to sell aspirins and hired bagpipers in full uniform and kilt to help. He despatched the bagpipers to a village and everyone from miles around came to see these strange men making these strange sounds. Then the selling began.

He told Matt Bishop of *F1 Racing:* 'I went from Dunlop to Aspro – headache pills – and I was overseas manager for Aspro.' It took him on a six-month trip to the Indian subcontinent and, having done his research, he concluded that the way to sell there was to take Aspro directly to the people.

'One of the problems with communicating the product benefits of Aspro was our inability to communicate with them, because they couldn't read and even if they could there were no newspapers. The basic way was to take advertising space on radio Ceylon, which was booked three years in advance.'

However ... in 'the course of our investigations we discovered that the Indians, as a race, are very keen on bagpipes. We recruited eight bagpipe-playing Indians.' When they'd finished playing, a ninth man – an Indian businessman – 'literally erected a folding soap box and said to the villagers "here I am, here today and gone tomorrow, and I'm here to tell you about Aspro. Have you got dandruff? Have you got piles? Do you get headaches? Ulcers? This is what you need ..."'

' . . . and Eddie Jordan is in fifth place '

Walker's motorsport commentating really did begin by chance, in 1948 at Shelsley Walsh near Worcester where there was, and still is, a famous hill-climb. This was of sufficient importance that Graham was due to commentate on it for the BBC but for some reason couldn't, so the man doing the public address moved up to replace him and Graham recommended Murray to do the public address. Murray reasoned that if he did the equivalent of a full-out *radio* commentary over the public address the BBC producer was bound to hear it and be impressed. The producer did and was.

In May 1949 Murray was part of the BBC team for the British Grand Prix at Silverstone. He was positioned at Stowe corner, the fast right-hander out in the country, and there witnessed a British driver, John Bolster, crash so heavily that Murray thought he was dead. Historian Doug Nye writes (in *The British Grand Prix 1926–1976*, Batsford) that Bolster's car 'rolled wildly over the straw bales and severely injured its half-ejected driver. He lay by the trackside for 25 minutes before the ambulance arrived, sparking a terrific controversy about the use of straw bales and the efficiency of Silverstone's medical services.'

' This is an interesting circuit because it has inclines, and not just up but down as well '

A month later Murray was commentating with his father at the Tourist Trophy on the Isle of Man and Les Graham, an Englishman who that season would become the first world 500cc motorcycle champion, braked so late where Murray was standing that he nearly wiped him away.

Rosemeyer had been killed during a record speed attempt on an autobahn some three months after Murray had seen him win the 1937 Donington Grand Prix. Bolster could easily have died at Murray's feet. The Isle of Man was a very dangerous place and would claim its victims year after year. Murray understood from the beginning that every moment in motorsport bears within it the ultimate risk and if you are to become involved in it you must accept this.

From Aspro he was 'headhunted' by the advertising agency McCann-Eriksson to take care of the Esso account and 'worked on that for a couple of years.' While he'd been with Aspro he'd come into contact with another advertising agency called Masius, Ferguson and a man there called Jack Wynne-Williams. He was 'an inspirational leader of men' and Murray was fully prepared to be inspired.

Mind you, the BBC once rang and asked him to commentate on a weight-lifting championship, a subject of which he knew as much, or as little, as you and I. He did what a resourceful man would do, rang the secretary of weight-lifting's governing body and offered to drive him to the championship. During the journey Murray found out all he needed to know. One part of his approach to commentating was already in place: meticulous research.

Commentating, however, was and would continue to be a weekend pastime. From 1951, the voice of motor-sport on the BBC was Raymond Baxter. 'When I first knew Murray he worked for Dunlop. I knew his father very well and when I first joined the Outside Broadcast Department of the BBC in London, one of my very early jobs was to be what we called in those days Number 2 to Graham at the TT on the Isle of Man. He was at the start-finish, Murray was out on the course and my principal job was to try and get Graham to shut up when the transmission time had come to an end.'

The years never touched the smile.

2

THE GROCERS OF
ST JAMES'S

'The company was called Masius, Ferguson – from a guy called Mike Masius, an American who worked in advertising before the war. He had a good war, came back to London, which he liked, and started an advertising agency with a guy called Fergie Ferguson. They became a very successful agency and shortly after that Jack Wynne-Williams came in as managing director.' The speaker, Eddie Stephens, worked there and so, as we have seen, did Murray Walker. Stephens charts the name changes: Masius-Ferguson became Masius, Wynne-Williams and then D'Arcy. 'This is an industry with lots of acronyms and initials but in Murray's time if he was asked where he worked he'd have said 'Masius'.

Here Murray worked from Monday to Friday every week from the 1950s until 1982. He was high-powered, he was happy, he found advertising a fascinating world – and he was 'lucky' enough (his word) to be successful.

The agency was based in St James's Square, just off Pall Mall in London, and thereby hangs a tale or two. As Stephens points out, 'St James's was very elegant and used to be known as the best address in London. In the 1950s, when agencies had particular reputations, J Walter Thompson was known as the University of Advertising and, because we had so many successful food accounts, we were known as the Grocers of St James's Square. So you could either be with the University or the Grocers and we were very proud of that. Murray would have been very proud of that too.

'When I joined in 1967 there were maybe 300 people working at the agency. It was a major concern. We had rapidly become one of the largest agencies in London, and we handled all the kind of accounts you'd expect a major agency to do – food, lots of packaged goods, Colgate, Palmolive, Mars, British Rail, General Motors – all the blue chip stuff. It was the beginning of television advertising and the kind of companies we dealt with tended to be major advertisers who went for the most appropriate medium so we were a pioneering television agency. Murray became a main board member. In advertising that is always a working director, and he worked the same hours as everybody else. He was an account executive – an outstandingly good account person, which is to say he was the person who represented the client to the agency. One enduring characteristic was that he always, always strove to find the fairest way forward. He was absolutely transparent and honest with his clients and his agency colleagues, and that was one of the reasons he was so admired. He was absolutely straight on everything.

'He was, oh, tremendously enthusiastic. One of the things about Murray is his irrepressible enthusiasm, the kind of thing which he has now become famous for in motorsport, but that was his personality here too. He is a natural enthusiast. Another thing about Murray: you will never find anybody who, if they are being honest with you, can tell you anything less than good about him. Murray is not one of those people who has got any bad stuff about him.

'One of the very nice things was the way he encouraged young people in a business where sometimes not everything goes right first time. No matter how junior you were, or whatever you had done, you could be sure that if Murray was your boss he would help you. He was sensationally good with younger people.

'He was proud of his father and the most prominent thing he had in his office was a picture of Graham in the TT races. His father competed on the Island and I think it was always Murray's dream to do that too. The picture was very important for him and it was taken from office to office as he moved. One of the memories of people who worked with him will always be that he used to have that smashing picture of his father.

'Remember in those days he wasn't anything like as public a figure or as well known as he has become. If you were his colleague or his client, the motor racing side of his life and his involvement in it wouldn't be the first thing that came up. He would talk about your business, or the client's business. He did his job here 100%. The last thing he'd tell you was "by the way, I do a lot of commentating." The discussion you would have with Murray would be a business one. He is a very focused man. He kept his two worlds quite separate and I respected his integrity in doing that. It's why he was such a good professional in both.

'When I listen to him now I am listening to the same man. He has not changed in the slightest. He has a lot of charm ...'

Masius were successful and Tony Jardine, who's known Murray for a couple of decades, reinforces what Stephens has said. 'Murray was a high-powered executive at the agency and one account he worked on was Babycham. They did so well on Babycham that, for a Christmas present, one of the big bosses of the agency got a Jack Barclay's folder with keys inside.' Jack Barclay sold Rolls-Royces and the keys were for a new one. 'That was the Christmas bonus.'

Jardine insists that Murray's time at the agency 'has made him such a complete bloke because he understands the cut and thrust of business, he understands the commercial side of things extremely well – better than most – which is also why you see him understanding Formula 1 so well. Formula 1 is a sport but it is also big business, of course, and he can see how the whole thing clicks, how it works.'

And now we come to a tale with a tweak in the tail feathers – budgies, and specifically two jingles: *Trill makes budgies bounce with health* and *An only budgie is a lonely budgie.*

Andrew Marriott, another media person who has known Murray for decades, recounts that 'when I first met him he used to talk about the advertising world but he kept it completely separate. He must have changed out of the pin stripe suit or whatever he wore, changed into sporting commentary clothes and off he went.

'As Murray tells me, one of his biggest accounts was pet foods owned by Mars and they had a product called Trill – for budgies. Big meeting at the agency, client's there. "We've got a problem with Trill: 97% of all people that buy budgie seed buy Trill so how can we increase the sales?" They dreamed up a budgie lovers' club of some description which had a motto *An only budgie is a lonely budgie.*'

The thinking behind this was simplicity itself. If you feel your budgie is lonely, you buy it a companion and you naturally feed the companion Trill too – doubling sales.

The problem with that, Marriott attests, was 'in those days, a lot of old ladies had budgies for company and the budgies would squawk back to them "hello, granny" or whatever. However when you get two budgies together they don't imitate English any more, they just squawk away to each other. It worked fine for Trill but the old ladies didn't have them squawking back ...'

And *Trill makes budgies bounce with health?* Yes, in those days it was a famous jingle and Jardine insists that Murray had a hand in it.

This leads to the *A Mars a day helps you work, rest and play* jingle which, to people of a certain age, still has a resonance. Although Murray worked on part of the Mars account – some of their confectionery brands – 'funnily enough Mars Bars were not one of them. People always come to me and ask "is it true that you thought of *A Mars a day*" and it's because they've read it somewhere and it's just been perpetuated. I keep on saying "no, it's not true that I thought of that."'

Murray married Elizabeth. Their eyes 'met across a room, quite literally, at a party and I decided there and then.' She was 27, he was 36 and 'I'd been around a bit, had the privilege of holding hands with a few women. It took us about four years – some to-ing and fro-ing and on-and-offing, but it's worked very well because we've been married for 40 years now.' They do not have children.

' With the race half gone there is still half the race to go '

Barrie Gill 'started doing TV and motor racing in about 1965. As far as television was concerned, motor racing was the Monaco Grand Prix – where they took snatches – and the British Grand Prix. And at that time, pre-Bernie Ecclestone, you never knew which teams would come. The organisers had to negotiate individually with each team, so there were always rumours that there'd been a sighting of a Ferrari down at Portsmouth or Dover. Incredible!

'Murray was a leading executive in the advertising world, a main board director at Masius responsible for the Dunlop account. In fact he launched the Groundhog tyre.

'When I was doing motor racing with Raymond Baxter, Murray was the guy holding a clip-board with information about the Formula 3s or the saloon cars because the Grand Prix drivers drove in three races. So Murray was this high-powered advertising guy who turned up on a motor bike – he went to every race on a motor bike, that's how he got there so quickly. He started off as a course commentator, a commentator on motor bikes and junior events. The stars did Formula 1.' Raymond Baxter confirms this. 'Murray didn't do any Grand Prix racing at all.' Baxter did it with three others.

Murray, however, covered the Isle of Man TT races in the 1960s, a time when Mike Hailwood became arguably the greatest rider who ever lived. Murray knew Hailwood and his millionaire father Stan well.

'Stan's house was fairly close to Silverstone and it was a tradition that when there was a big meeting there, if my father and I were doing the commentary, Stan would invite us to stay. The cynic in me suggests that Stan was asking us not only because my father was editor of *Motor Cycling* and therefore not at all a bad bloke to be on the right side of, but because Graham and Murray Walker could give an extra amount of publicity to his gifted son. It worked, because I'm damn sure we did it without realising it.'

' *We're now on the 73rd lap, and the next one will be the 74th* '

Here is an interview that Murray did with Mike Hailwood on the Island in 1967. It shows how, although he had no training as a journalist, he understood the true mechanisms of interviewing: you don't impose yourself on the subject, you enable them to tell their story. The interview took place after the 500cc race, one of the most astonishing ever run. Hailwood, a handsome sex symbol, was racing against Giacomo Agostini, another handsome sex symbol. They were easily the two best riders in the world. During the race Hailwood's twist grip on the handlebars came loose, a terrifying situation around the Island with its ditches, stone walls and houses. Agostini broke down.

Walker: Mike, you are the first TT winner that I have ever seen clutching a bunch of flowers and smelling them. How do you feel after that?

Hailwood: I feel a bit of a twit holding these things! I'm a bit tired naturally. It was a very, very hard race.

Walker: Mike, have you ever had as hard a race as that anywhere?

Hailwood: Er … I think probably last year might have been the equal of it but I don't know really.

Walker: Well tell me something about it. What happened on the first lap, because you were 12 seconds down on Agostini.

Hailwood: Yes.

Walker: Did you have a bad first lap?

Hailwood: Every lap was bad [laughs] but no, actually I didn't expect to be in the lead. I didn't expect to win at all today, actually. Secretly.

Walker: Now what was it, was it machine handling trouble?

Hailwood: Yeah. Mostly.

Walker: But yet on the second lap – when you went round at 108.77mph, in case you don't know, and broke the previous lap record – you dragged that lead down to just over eight seconds. How much harder were you trying on that second lap?

Hailwood: A lot harder – well, no, I wasn't actually, I had got more used to the machine.

Walker: Now when you came in, Mike, to the pit I couldn't see you but you were hammering at something.

Hailwood: Yes.

Walker: What was the trouble?

Hailwood: Well, the throttle kept falling off, sliding off, so I thought if I hit the end of this it would stop it sliding off, you know, but apparently the bit I was hitting was all attached to the throttle anyway so it still kept coming off.

Walker: And you still had this trouble all through the rest of the race?

Hailwood: It was only coming off slowly up until the last lap and on the last lap it was so loose it fell off once in actual fact.

Walker: Which accounts for your last lap going down by some seven miles an hour.

Hailwood: Yes. Well, I couldn't do anything else except hold it on. I was riding virtually one-handed.

(Andy Marriott feels that 'Murray's an even better motorcycling commentator than racing car commentator. He knew the techniques of riding because he'd grown up with it.')

' MURRAY'S MOMENTS
Tony Jardine, ITV broadcaster and PR man

Murray hadn't been to the cinema in absolutely yonks – you'd be talking about Gone with the Wind *or something like that! Jim Rosenthal had been talking about* Gladiator *and how great it was, we arrived in Canada and it was on down the road. I said "let's go" and eventually he said "all right." The cinema was quite full and* Gladiator *was being shown with big sound surround.*

When Murray's around it's the noise that he makes: he's among racing engines, he's impervious to it all, he'll put his head next to a V12 and go "WONDER-FUL, WONDER-FUL!"

The opening half an hour of Gladiator *batters the senses in the sound surround and Murray was muttering "Christ." About 40 minutes in there's the romantic scene and the cinema went absolutely silent but Murray had forgotten that the noise level had dropped. "THAT'S BLOODY SOPPY, ISN'T IT?" Everyone was watching him and he was saying "sorry, sorry."*

To which journalist Gerry Donaldson adds: "Murray bellows. If he wants to raise his voice nobody can do it louder. It's like an earth tremor." '

It's easy to forget how much the world has changed. As Gill says, Grand Prix racing scarcely existed on television and the working conditions were primitive. 'What people don't realise is that in those days all the monitors were black and white. You'd be sitting watching, something's happening round the other side of Spa and you'd say "and I think it's a Ferrari" – you didn't know it was red.

'To do the Monaco Grand Prix you sat on benches with the cars about a yard away from you, whether

❛ MURRAY'S MOMENTS
Roger Moody, former BBC producer

The only time I used to get terribly frustrated was at his inability to stop talking. There was a school of thought at the BBC that the pictures could tell the story and the commentary was only there to add on – but of course that is not Murray's modus operandi. Frequently when I was alongside him I'd push my button and say "stop talking, Murray" or hold a piece of paper up in front of him so he couldn't see the track.

He'd look at me through those owl-like spectacles and he'd be thinking "what is this idiot doing?" However it would cause him to stop and I thought "I've cracked it!" Within two seconds he was off at enormous, express train-like pace again and it was impossible to stop him then. ❜

it was raining or not, and you had to do a lap chart – there was no screen telling you who was where. There was a commentary going on over the public address in French sometimes, Italian sometimes, and you only had this one view of the track in front of you. You were covering the race with a much worse view of it than the person sitting at home. I've seen Murray sitting there, soaking wet, shouting above the noise of the cars, with a producer behind him trying to keep a wet lap chart up to date. The conditions were frankly unbelievable but that's the way it was.

'You have to remember the BBC switched off motor racing because the cars carried advertising. In 1976, for example, the only coverage of the British Grand Prix with James Hunt challenging for the World Championship was coverage we [Gill's company] made for ITV – we made this movie and got 25 minutes on ITV. Then the championship went to Japan [Mount Fuji, where Hunt won] and I did the commentary for television in Japan. Murray was back in the studio in London and he put a commentary over what they put out in the afternoon. James got motor racing back on air and by that time Murray was the commentator.'

It happened like this. One Monaco Grand Prix, Walker sat trackside with, he explains, 'an open line telling Raymond Baxter what was going on.' Baxter, of course, was the commentator and in London. 'He could ask me questions and I could give him answers. Cars crashed on the first lap, general mayhem, and about four laps into the race the landlines between Paris and Monaco went down. As a result the communication between me in Monaco and Raymond Baxter in London was lost.

'Raymond sat looking at pictures of a race he couldn't fathom because of the crashes, and the resultant broadcast was, I understand, not very good. It wasn't any fault of Raymond's because he sat at the sharp end doing the best job he could in the circumstances. When it was decided that in 1977 the BBC would create a programme called *Grand Prix,* Jonathan Martin [Head of Sport] asked me to do the races. I don't imagine Raymond would have wanted to because he'd done motor racing and was a big man in other spheres.'

Baxter did not agree. He loved motor racing, 'every second of it. One of the big influences in why I had to give it up was because I left the BBC and became director of publicity at the British Motor Corporation. My intention at that time was gradually to ease my way out of broadcasting and try to carve a serious career in the motor industry. Then Lord Stokes won the battle for BMC and I was the first person he sacked.'

By this stage Murray was in full flow.

Raymond Baxter had a genteel, soothing, sophisticated voice in absolute contrast to Murray. 'It is a question of individual style,' Baxter says. 'I got just as excited, I think – in fact I'm sure – but I tried to keep an outward aura of calm without being boring. The whole thing was much more disciplined. That's the way we were taught broadcasting.'

In 1978 the BBC decided to do all 16 races. Whatever else such a move brought, it was going to deliver an awful lot of Murray Walker. Initially there was viewer resistance. Some people, as Simon Taylor says, didn't like Murray's excitable delivery and felt how unsuitable it all was. 'They couldn't stand him, particularly the enthusiasts. What is so remarkable about Murray is that he has come from a position where in the early days he was almost reviled – hugely criticised and people used to write to *Autosport* saying how ghastly it was and so on – but what Murray did, absolutely correctly, was ignore the criticism and simply carry on doing what he did. He didn't alter his style, he didn't alter his approach because like all great commentators he was doing it in a totally genuine, unforced way. What you heard with Murray was Murray and you either liked it or you didn't. And gradually everybody came to love it.'

Soon enough you would begin to feel you knew him personally. And, as it happened, that was just the beginning, never mind that within a couple of years he thought his position was under such threat that it was the end.

They both had hold of the microphone . . .

3

THEN ALONG CAME HUNT

In 1979, James Hunt was driving for the Wolf team, his career virtually over. He decided to retire in mid-season and did so after the Monaco Grand Prix. Barrie Gill, running the PR company CSS, was asked to handle the announcement. Gill did that and also said to Jonathan Martin 'well, how about him doing the TV?'

Gill remembers that 'they tried James at Silverstone on, I suppose, a Formula 5000 race. For some reason his leg was in plaster so he lay on the floor and afterwards he said to me "that's the most boring thing I've ever seen in my life!"' It might have been boring but it led to another life because Martin decided to hire him.

Martin would say 'I'd come into contact with him a bit because in 1977 and 1978 we were all over the European circuits and he was what I would call a focused chap, abrupt from time to time and friendly at other times. I didn't feel it represented a risk in the sense that we could already see from his interviews – because he wasn't new to it, he'd been interviewed a lot – that he was a communicator.'

James Hunt was 33, an ex public schoolboy with a cavalier (let us say) approach to whichever life he happened to be living at the time. He would be forever famous for being World Champion in 1976. He'd won and lost beautiful women, he'd taken drugs and often dressed like a hippie. He liked drink, cigarettes, irreverence and doing what he wanted how he wanted.

Murray Walker was old enough to be Hunt's father, an ex tank commander with a highly disciplined (let us say) approach to life. He worked regular hours in the advertising agency. He was punctual, conscientious and always well dressed. He liked wine in moderation, didn't smoke, was reverent and accustomed to doing things as they should be done. He had what he'd describe as a 'puritanical background'.

Murray suspected that Hunt found him a 'boring old so-and-so' and he certainly regarded Hunt as a Hooray Henry. It was a recipe for disaster. Worse, Murray's reaction when Jonathan Martin told him there would now be two commentators was 'fear and resentment – fear that he'd replace me and I'd lose a job I loved, resentment that I knew how long it took to learn to commentate.'

Roger Moody, who'd be producing the duet, 'joined the BBC in 1970 – Radio Birmingham, where I was their first sports producer. Ironically enough James, who was at the height of his driving fame in the 1970s, came into the studios and I interviewed him. When James decided to retire and the BBC hired him we all thought it was wonderful but for me it was like James coming home, having originally met him at Pebble Mill. I think we were all slightly concerned at how he would get on with Murray and it's well documented that at the start it was quite an uneasy relationship.

'I was determined that James would try to be a little bit more than the playboy he often portrayed. I'd say to him "now listen, I want you to walk up and down the pit lane before a race and get all the information, then come into the commentary box when Murray does." And of course what happened? James would amble in at the last moment, which used to drive me mad and drive Murray absolutely frantic. Bear in mind that Murray and I would get up at something like five o'clock in the morning to beat the traffic into the circuit. James would arrive maybe four or five hours later and you could only ever find him in the Marlboro McLaren motorhome smoking and drinking – usually Coca-Cola, to be fair to him. He wouldn't budge out of there and he would not get any pit lane gossip because basically it all came to him in the McLaren motorhome anyway or, if he did work for it, he did that in a very unconventional way.

'Then – and this is where Murray and I would be frantic sitting up in the commentary box – the London studios would be saying "we're coming to you now for the warm-up lap." Murray would look at me and mouth *where is James?* I'd shrug. We knew where he was but we had no idea when he was going to turn up. Murray would start the warm-up lap and then, metaphorically, he'd throw his microphone to one side and mouth at me again *WHERE IS JAMES???* I'd say 'keep going Murray, I've no idea.' As the cars came round after the formation lap and were coming to a halt before the green light James would enter, sometimes without any shoes on. He might be wearing cut-off jeans, all tatty, a tatty tee-shirt, and have a fag hanging out of his mouth, a can of Coke in his hand. He'd just plonk himself down and Murray would "throw" something to him and James was off instantly. To be fair, it always worked like clockwork. Murray was relieved, as I was, that James had turned up.

'James only let the side down once, in Belgium one year. He allegedly had food poisoning. It was raining hard throughout the race and we dragged a succession of drivers who'd dropped out for various reasons up to the commentary box, so instead of having Murray plus James we had Murray plus about ten different drivers.'

Keith Mackenzie, one of Moody's successors, would also confront Hunt's notions of timekeeping. 'I can remember Monaco one year, I suppose we were about 15 minutes away from going on the air and *WHERE IS JAMES???* Off I went to search for him and I found him wandering from the harbour – where he'd spent the weekend on a boat – through the pit lane onto the grid, no shoes, socks or anything. It was almost as if he'd just got out of bed. That was not the sort of thing which endeared him to Murray, or Mr Ecclestone either. Murray would never have said a cross word against James and it was never apparent to the viewer – you wouldn't know the real situation. Everybody who listened to the commentary thought they were the best of mates. In fact they had very little to do with each other.'

(To be fair to Hunt, Barrie Gill is sure that 'James used to wind Murray up by deliberately staying outside the commentary box. I'd be going off down to the pits and it was *WHERE IS JAMES??? WHERE IS HE???* He was outside having a smoke or whatever and he'd just wander in. It was a game and he loved it!')

Punctuality was not the only source of friction. Both men liked to have the microphone and both felt that, at any given moment, they were entitled to have it.

Murray 'did like to hog the microphone and the one time he was frustrated was when James got behind it,' Moody says. 'Murray would be twitchy. You could see him wanting to get it himself, see he was determined to get back behind it. I can remember him saying "come on James, come on James, give me the microphone, I've got to commentate on this" – *you are stealing my thunder, James.* And James would just keep on going, fag in one hand, microphone in the other.'

'James and Murray were so competitive and combative that they had one microphone to make sure they wouldn't talk over each other,' Barrie Gill says. 'I have seen it again and again: James wrapped the wire round his arm so Murray couldn't get the microphone off him.'

All this represented anxiety for Moody. 'Occasionally I used to take my wife with me and she'd sit at the back of the box. She said "I have never ever seen you so stressed and tense in trying to get the show on the road." In those days the Press facilities were very archaic and the running of the television facilities equally archaic. You were trying to get the commentary box in the best position, you were trying to get your unilateral interviews back to London ahead of the French broadcaster, the Italian broadcaster, the Dutch broadcaster and so on getting the line. Now couple it with the fact that James wasn't as reliable as Murray and it all added up to stress, although ultimately everything worked perfectly.'

From it, from the contradictions and contrasts, Walker and Hunt became one of the great double acts and Walker himself became a genuine celebrity. He was intoxicated by every race, childlike in wonder in the presence of drivers and cars, almost completely uncritical. Hunt was monotone, acerbic and so forthright that he was unafraid to humiliate drivers. Murray, Moody says, appreciated James's comments and they were 'complete foils for each other.' The double act had – Moody's word – chemistry.

'With the greatest respect, and I'm terribly biased, I don't think there's ever been a combination quite like it. Martin Brundle has been tremendous but James had one thing Martin won't ever have. James had been World Champion, and of course he had that terrific playboy aura about him too. But during a race James could see things that no-one else could. I could never see whether a tyre was blistered or not. Murray would say "well there you are, he's slowing down, his wheel's coming off or his engine's about to blow up" and James would say "well actually, Murray, it's because …"'

'That was why it was so essential to have a driver alongside Murray, who's never driven a Formula 1 car apart from when it's been staged – and, when he has, he usually stalls it.'

Not that everything was smooth. 'There were occasions,' Moody says, 'when Murray would "throw" to James – Murray would be concentrating on either the monitor or the statistics or the race evolving in front of him, and he wouldn't be looking at James. There'd be deathly silence. Murray would look at James and I would look at James and James would be asleep! He would nod off occasionally – it was either a very boring race or a very good lunch. I remember the Paul Ricard circuit and the local Bandol rosé!'

Commentary boxes could be hot. 'James would come in virtually naked and in fact once we were all in there it was like being in a sauna. Murray and James were both stripped off, Murray down to the waist and doing his usual standing up bit. I don't think James was asleep this time but Murray was getting so frenetic that the sweat was flying all over the place like a hose. It was all dripping down onto James, who was completely oblivious to it. He didn't give a stuff!'

In 1982, Murray decided to leave advertising and concentrate on commentating. He once told me that he was sitting at the agency and wondered what he was doing there because he'd earned enough to be comfortable and was in a position to devote his time to his love of motor racing. Until then it had been, in a sense, a hobby. Linda Pattisson, who works for CSS and has advised and helped him for many years, sums it up neatly. 'It was only a case of stop one and do the other full-time.'

He could afford to. Years before, he and three other ambitious 'young' men were constantly badgering

Wynne-Williams about the business, suggesting how it could be improved. Wynne-Williams called them in one day in 1959 and said he'd had enough of it and was now going to give them a chance to 'put your money where your mouth is.' Murray remembers him saying 'I'll sell you each a percentage of the business – I want thirty thousand quid from each of you.' It was a fortune in 1959 but Murray borrowed it from the bank and after that 'I invested every spare penny I had got in the business. And every year to 1982, when I left, was a record year. I think our billing when I started was £1m and £1bn

'There's nothing wrong with the car except it's on fire!'

worldwide when I finished. I wasn't responsible for all of that but I helped it to happen and I had a very enjoyable, satisfying, rewarding business life.'

Eddie Stephens remembers going to his leaving party. 'It was a hilarious party but one of the most affectionate and caring I ever went to. He was a man universally admired. Did he get drunk at the party? No, no. He wasn't a drinker.'

'The thing that impressed me about Murray Walker,' former Formula 1 driver Julian Bailey will say, 'was when I won the Formula Ford Festival [at Brands Hatch] in 1982 and he was there. He's not just a Formula 1 enthusiast, he's actually a motor racing enthusiast. He's interested in the ladder – from the bottom to the top. That's one of his great strengths: his depth of knowledge of loads of drivers at early ages. He's known them for years. Murray wasn't commentating at Brands, he was wandering around having a chat with the drivers. He was already very famous then and I couldn't believe the guy took the time to be there. He said "hello Julian, how are you, I'm Murray Walker" as if he had to introduce himself. I've bumped into him all over the world since and we'll sit and have a meal, a glass of wine. He's one of those people I've known all my career.'

One decision would have to be made eventually, because the 16 Grands Prix were consuming so much of his time. He felt he could not do the British Bike Grand Prix justice. Keith Mackenzie 'first worked with Murray in 1986 at Silverstone doing the bike Grand Prix, which he did every year. That was the only one the BBC did, not all the other rounds. After a number of years, and because of that, he felt it was a bit of a strain to have to find out everything about the different categories, the 125s and the 500s and the sidecars and so on. I rang him one year and said "would you do the commentary?" and he said "really I think I'm going to give it away."'

Mark Wilkin, a producer who succeeded Moody in 1989, faced the familiar problem of James. 'Murray puts motor racing drivers on a pedestal and Grand Prix drivers on the highest step of that pedestal. James was clearly on that because he'd been a World Champion too. Murray felt threatened in the early days at James's arrival because he thought the idea was that James was going to replace him. There had only been one commentator, why should they suddenly want two? But Jonathan Martin's idea was always to make them into a team and that was absolutely the right decision.

'James, however, was a free spirit and largely uncontrollable in terms of the usual norms. Producers are very definitely in charge of programmes. We became very close after four years, five years. We'd see each other socially outside the races and we came to have an understanding that he wouldn't do things unless I'd OKd them. Having said that he *was* a free spirit and he wanted to have his share of the commentary.

'The first race I did with him I confiscated a bottle of red wine as he walked in the commentary box and replaced it with a bottle of water. He didn't notice. By the end of his time commentating he'd discovered the Press Room, he'd discovered lap charts were done and they'd give him vast amounts of information. He grew up.'

Wilkin found that Murray was 'a fantastic bloke. He was like a father, he was like your favourite teacher and he was such an enthusiast. He was bursting to tell you the stories. I remember that first time at Monaco I said

"I'm going to walk round the track" – I'd seen it on the telly but I'd never been there. He said "I'll come with you."'

He gave Wilkin the equivalent of a running commentary. '"This is *Rascasse*, this is Casino Square" and everywhere we stopped there was a story. "This is where so-and-so had his big crash at *Ste Devote*." He obviously knew everybody in the paddock and he introduced you. He was always looking after all of us. People would invite him and he'd say "I come as a team – my producer comes too." That's how he always operated.'

Grand Prix was becoming a much more complete programme. 'By the time I'd started we had moved the production on and we hired a cameraman for an hour or so. It was the first year of trying to do something more than just commentate on the race. We'd do a couple of bits for the highlights show, some preview stuff and some post-race stuff.

' . . . and in front of David Coulthard the scarlet McLaren of four times Monaco Grand Prix winner Michael Schumacher '

That was the first time Murray had had to do anything other than just commentary. Now he was doing interviews, doing what we call stand-ups – it's presenting to camera, an introductory piece saying "hello and welcome to Montreal" or whatever.

'We had to make sure we told the stories. That first race I went to at Monaco was after Berger's crash at Imola when he caught fire and everybody said "how on earth did he manage to get out of that?" My brief was fill the two-minute preview with something interesting. I thought the most interesting thing was how come Berger didn't die? It seemed obvious to go to Jonathan Palmer – Doctor Jonathan Palmer – and he talked us round the various safety measures. That was really when my relationship with Jonathan was born and it came to fruition a couple of years later.' Palmer was the BBC's man in the pit lane during races.

With Hunt, there were danger zones, particularly over the Italian driver Riccardo Patrese. He and Hunt had collided at the start of the 1978 Italian Grand Prix at Monza, and Hunt had then collided with Ronnie Peterson who subsequently died. Patrese was vilified and forever thereafter you were entitled to wonder about the motivation of Hunt's verbal assaults on him.

Wilkin remembers 'a classic case' of that. 'It was at Kyalami in 1992. Murray said something about Patrese, James jumped on the Patrese bandwagon and did his usual stuff. I hit the button and said "right, James, that's enough about Patrese" because it was very dangerous.'

(Barrie Gill ruminates on how acerbic Hunt really could be. 'The James and Murray Show was incredible because Murray is a kind man, Murray loves the drivers and Murray appreciates what they are going through, then James would say "de Cesaris shouldn't be allowed out" – and said it because he really felt it.')

Wilkin witnessed one of the very rare occasions when Murray lost his composure: Donington in 1993 and the European Grand Prix. 'It had been a difficult weekend, cold and miserable. The only good thing you could say was that we weren't at Aida [the remote, unloved Japanese circuit], which is why we were at Donington. Things had been difficult in the commentary box for a while.

'And I interrupt myself to bring you this'

'They'd come to me in 1992, both of them individually. James said "I've been thinking about it and I've got to say something. I think Murray is getting more than his share. I'm not getting enough of the commentary." I said "well, James, you're absolutely right. I've been listening and I've been thinking about it. You know Murray's difficult – he wants to talk the whole race. I'll have a word with Murray and I'll redress the balance." About an hour later Murray came to me and said "you know, I've been thinking that James is getting more than his share." I said "well, Murray, you're absolutely right. I'll have a word with him and I'll make sure it's sorted out." I didn't say a word to either of them and after the next race they both said "I don't know what you said but it was very effective. Thanks very much."

'At Donington it came to a head and I don't really know why. Possibly it was because there is more pressure at British rounds and Murray gets mobbed wherever he goes. That may have had something to do with it – he never likes to say "no" to anybody and it

MURRAY'S MOMENTS
Roger Moody, former BBC producer

The first Spanish Grand Prix of the modern era, 1986, was at Jerez, and we arrived on the Thursday. The Spanish are typically laid back. We went to our allocated commentary box and there was the smallest black and white monitor you can imagine. Murray said "well, I can't possibly work with that" – and he couldn't.

We said we needed a big colour monitor: coloured cars going to 180 miles an hour you can't identify on the monitor they'd provided. They said they couldn't do anything about it and I said "OK, we'll fly a monitor out from England."

When we arrived on race day there was the biggest colour television I have laid eyes on – it completely filled the box. They must have taken it from some high-ranking executive's office.

Murray used to stick his charts and his information all around the box but he didn't have anywhere to stick anything because this monitor was so big and he certainly couldn't look over the top of it. He coped with that very professionally.

really upset him if people wanted his autograph and he had to be somewhere at a certain time. But once he stopped he'd be surrounded.'

Possibly it was because the race in wet-dry-wet-dry conditions was deeply chaotic with so many pit stops and crashes that following its narrative was extremely difficult.

'Anyway we were in the commentary box and whenever James was talking Murray would be agitated – standing up – and he'd be desperate to get the microphone. Something happened. James decided to ignore him and the picture cut to an overtaking or a near overtaking. James thought he'd carry on with whatever he was saying. Murray felt the point wasn't interesting enough and he grabbed the microphone off James. He started to talk and with that James stood up and grabbed the microphone. They both had hold of the microphone, which has a long handle. They were going like *this* [tug-of-war] and Murray got his hand up like *this* and was ready to punch James. With that I've leapt up from my position and gone in boxing referee style – I couldn't say anything because the microphone was still on. I put my finger up and looked at them both and shook my head. They suddenly realised *what on earth are we doing* and carried on the commentary.'

The irony is that by now the relationship within the double act had altered towards great affection. Before one race at Imola they had dined together and Murray wondered which wine James would like. James said he had given up drinking – and had. 'I've had my share,' he said. From that moment, Murray insists, James became 'all the better a bloke for it because underneath he was an extremely warm-hearted, kind, friendly, sharp-minded nice chap. That's what he became, a genuinely loving father who would bring his kids to the hotel in Portugal every year when we did the Grand Prix there and he was marvellous, marvellous.' Hunt also took his duties as a commentator more seriously in terms of gathering information and so on.

'Do my eyes deceive me or is Senna's car sounding a bit rough?'

Keith Mackenzie says 'it's quite true that listening you would not know that any of the early friction was happening. It was a very professional relationship in the commentary box and that's more or less where it started and finished. Then I remember being at the South African Grand Prix with James [in 1993] and we all said "really James is starting to get himself together at last" but it was obviously too late by then. He'd done too much damage.'

He had.

James wrapped the wire round his arm . . .

4

A WORD IN EDGEWAYS

James Hunt died of a heart attack on 15 June 1993. Compounding the sense of complete shock was the fact that he had commentated quite normally on the Canadian Grand Prix two days before. It seemed impossible that the gravel-bed voice was gone forever. He was 45 and left a widow and two young sons. Roger Moody gives an epitaph in simple, direct words. 'Murray and I and everyone grew to love James and we were all desperately sad when he went so early.'

Amid the sadness and mourning, the BBC had to face an immediate problem: coverage of the French Grand Prix at Magny-Cours on 4 July. Jonathan Palmer was 'running a corporate event' at a small track called Bruntingthorpe. 'I had a phone call from Mark Wilkin to say James had died. I was in the hospitality unit when I took the call and was absolutely stunned. We all were. It was a bit like when a racing driver has been killed and you get the call from the team. When do you stop saying "how tragic" and "how awful" and say "what about it, who's going to do the job?" Mark is a straightforward bloke and he felt, I think, that I was the best person to take over the role. It was a fairly tense time and it was only three or four days before Mark came back and said "you're in the hot seat for Magny-Cours." It would have been difficult taking over from James anyway, but more difficult because of the circumstances. It wasn't as if James had retired at the end of a year and I'd been chosen amongst a whole load of potential candidates. I was there by default because it was right in the middle of the year. I knew the systems a bit and I had obviously worked with Murray and James in the pit lane. I hadn't commentated.'

Wilkin judges that 'Jonathan had a very, very difficult job when he started, especially trying to fill James's shoes after 13 years and in those circumstances. Jonathan was going to be compared with James – and compared with James after his thirteenth year, which was terribly unfair but a fact. Jonathan is a very bright man and he knew that people would compare him. He was very concerned about it.'

'I was very, very eager to do it,' Palmer says. 'I did France and I must admit I was absolutely terrified. I was amazed how different it was actually being there and having the microphone in front of you. It was something which, as a job, I got better and better at. I think Martin

Brundle does a better job than I did at it but he does it in a slightly different way. He's less technical, he's less intellectual about it, he's more off the cuff and probably more relaxed.'

Before the French Grand Prix coverage began Murray, sombre, found the mood. He said to camera: 'Today at Magny-Cours is going to be a sad experience for me and for you – the first Grand Prix without my partner for the past 13 years, James Hunt. It isn't going to be easy for any of us. We'll miss his wit and his wisdom.'

After the race coverage, *Grand Prix* showed a pre-recorded tribute from Murray. He sat by a fountain wearing a white shirt and a tie but no jacket. It was, consciously or not, just the right blend, neither too formal nor informal. James, after his reformation, would certainly have approved.

Murray, speaking slowly and with his emotions barely contained, explained how closely their working lives had become interwoven: 'For 16 weekends a year for the last 13 years, from Australia to Brazil to Mexico to South Africa to America – that was how closely James and I used to work together. Because of that we got to know each other pretty well and I very rapidly discovered that James was a very special sort of person. He didn't think the way other people do, he certainly didn't act the way other people do and he was always very exciting, stimulating and fun – unpredictable but a very authoritative person. In fact it was very obvious to everybody from his very earliest days that whatever James chose to do in later life he was going to make a success of it.'

Shortly after Hunt's death I was writing a biography of him (*Portrait of a Champion*, PSL 1993) and telephoned Murray for the story of their partnership. Although I knew both men and had been, I suppose, reasonably close to the currents and cross currents of Grand Prix racing since 1982, what happened next was revealing on two levels. First, Murray said 'this is the interview I really don't want to give.' It was strange for someone usually so helpful. He weighed it up for a long moment or two and said *OK, I'll tell you the story*. I had no idea of the enormous strains between them in the early days. Murray, the ultimate communicator, had never as far as I am aware communicated the friction to anyone outside the tiny BBC circle of *Grand Prix*, who could see it for themselves. For years he showed the perfect discretion of a gentleman.

Now, with me seeking to know, he felt he should either tell the truth or say nothing at all. That was the second level. He was not prepared to deal in hypocrisy and told it as it had been, not sparing himself either.

He sincerely missed Hunt and we all did. The gravel-bed voice *had* gone forever. Palmer was altogether more circumspect, polite and proper, even as he learnt to commentate and to partner Murray.

Murray in the garden, aged 3, already showing his presence to camera and preparing, no doubt, to make that pedal car Go, Go, GO!

The first love was motor bikes. Murray on a Rudge in Douglas, Isle of Man, at the age of 9 pretending to win the TT. For a crash helmet he has his schoolboy cap and for protection – bare knees.

Graham Walker, Murray's father, in 1931 on a 250cc bike with, immediately behind him, his wife Elsie. He won the Lightweight TT and, at 15st 3lbs, is believed to be the heaviest winner ever at the Isle of Man. (Mick Woollett)

Below, left: *Murray in 1946 when he was a captain and technical adjutant of the Royal Scots Greys.*

Below, right: *The advertising executive in 1949, with Dunlop's tyre division. In advertising 'he was absolutely transparent and honest' – and worked office hours just like everybody else.*

In the 1960s you might see Murray at minor circuits enjoying himself. Here he is at Hawkstone Park in 1960. (Nick Nicholls)

Murray interviews Mike Hailwood and Derek Minter at Brands Hatch in 1960. (Nick Nicholls)

Murray Walker and James Hunt became a great double act. (Formula One Pictures)

Preparing to interview Derek Warwick and Kenny Acheson ... (Formula One Pictures)

... while BBC producer Roger Moody keeps a watchful eye from behind the sunglasses. (Formula One Pictures)

The new partnership which was a forced succession to Hunt and Walker: Jonathan Palmer and Walker. (Palmer Sport)

Martin Brundle remembers that as a driver he didn't know Murray particularly well. (Formula One Pictures)

Above, left: *Striding with his military gait.* (Formula One Pictures)

Above: *The days when Grand Prix racing, the BBC and Murray Walker seemed wedded forever.* (Formula One Pictures)

Left: With Sir Stirling Moss and wife Susie at the annual *Autosport* awards. (LAT)

Britain's Grand Prix drivers say goodbye to Murray and the BBC, from left: Damon Hill, David Coulthard, Martin Brundle and Johnny Herbert. (Sporting Pictures UK Ltd)

Murray received the OBE in 1996 and Damon Hill seems suitably impressed. (ICN UK Bureau)

The new world at ITV in 1997 – left to right, Tony Jardine, Jim Rosenthal, Martin Brundle, Murray, Louise Goodman and James Allen. (ITV)

Stand and deliver – side by side with Martin Brundle. (LAT)

'To start with we had one microphone because that's the way James and Murray had done it and that was the way Mark Wilkin had wanted it done – otherwise they would talk over each other. Fairly soon I was very keen to have separate microphones. It was cumbersome changing from one to the other and difficult to get it off Murray! It was a lot better when you had your own microphone and just put your hand up if you wanted to talk. I'm not saying it was necessarily easy like that but, the way it now worked, he could keep possession of his microphone without feeling that he had lost it for an indeterminate period by giving it away.'

Palmer also had to learn the delicate art of pointing out Murray's blunders, some thundering and some quieter – a sensitive issue, not least because Murray was following the race at racing speed while Palmer, as Hunt had before him, was essentially observing it and that gave him an enormous advantage in weighing his words.

'To start with, something worth saying is that people who haven't commentated have no idea how difficult it is watching what's going on and talking coherently, logically, clearly and interestingly about it. There's no going back, there's no changing your words, you can't *um* and *er* and it's hard work.

'To watch something, be thinking about it, analysing it and talking about it is a bit like a translator: you've got to be doing it all at once. The other big pressure is having people stand on every word you say. If you say anything stupid – and of course we all do from time to time – people are very quick to ridicule and mock. I used to let some things go. I don't think I was as quick to correct as Martin – Martin has a level of confidence and relationship where he is blunter. I'd always endeavour to keep corrections polite.

'I did enjoy working with Murray very much. We got on well and still do. Inevitably if you have a close working relationship there are times when there is a bit of friction but I'm sure Murray has it with everyone and every commentator has it, particularly when you're in a competitive environment. It's a bit like being a long-distance sportscar driver: both drivers want to be driving the car all the time, both want to do that bit more, and in a commentary box everyone thinks that what they have to say is more important than what the other guy has to say.

'Friction? We had the odd *frisson* of frustration and anger between us I'm sure – both ways – but that's the nature of the beast. Certainly we never ever had any kind of rows or anything which we needed to sort out after-wards. The nearest I can remember to Murray getting annoyed, then angry, with me when I wasn't aware of it happened when we were doing the Hungarian Grand Prix. It was a race where pit stops were prevalent – two or three pit stops – and one of those times in the race when it was important to explain to the viewer what we were looking at now. "The options here are Schumacher could be pitting in the next three laps and, if he doesn't, that means the lead Hill's got is going to carry him to the end of the race." That sort of thing.

'I was off on my train of thought on that, going through the tortuous but relatively important points which needed going through. While I was doing it I knew that Murray would half listen. He started waving his hand in front of me. Our signal was that if either of us wanted to take over you'd hold your hand in front and if it was urgent you'd wave it. I was about half way through making my point when Murray started waving. I looked at the screen and there was nothing really going on so I continued, because I wanted to finish and I couldn't have come back to it.

'There was another 20 seconds of dialogue from me and he was getting *so* agitated. Eventually, and I'll never forget it, he put his microphone down on the table and crossed his arms and stood there. When I did finish he looked across and glared at me very pointedly. He waited a bit then picked up the microphone and carried on. That was as near as it got.

'He is very competitive, a bit of a Jekyll and Hyde. He does have this avuncular sort of approach to all and sundry outside of the working environment but when you're in that environment working with him he is pretty feisty in his way, whether it's with the producers or whoever. He can change quickly from being easy-going to being pretty hard. He does care and he is competitive too. He was competitive in his commentary. He wanted to be talking and he'd want to make the important points. Our roles complemented each other very well. I was much more careful to recognise the obligations of my patch, if you like, as determined by my producer. I enjoyed trying to help the viewer understand more about what he or she was watching.

'We would normally dine together and he was charming company. He was very astute as well. He came over as much sharper on all sorts of issues over a casual dinner conversation, quite a worldly individual with very interesting and sometimes quite polarised opinions on an awful lot of matters. To some extent that contrasted with the slightly bumbling mistake-ridden persona that we saw on television. He was celebrated for some major blunders but part of that is that he does so much and he's been commentating for so long. Outside of that, over lunch or dinner, he's a very bright bloke. People would be surprised just how sharp Murray is.

'It hadn't ever occurred to me to have an opinion whether he would or wouldn't be aware of other things. There was a lot of conversation about motorsport but as much that wasn't about motorsport. We had debates and a lot of fun.

'As a commentator you felt very reassured having Murray alongside you because if you ever dried up you could rely on him to take over and there wouldn't be a nasty pregnant pause and fingers pointing back at you to continue. He was always a safety net. Also when dreadful things happened, like the Senna accident, his natural ability to feel the mood and express it was unique and outstanding. No-one will ever emulate him overall but the biggest area they will never do that in is having such genuine feelings of emotion and relaying those feelings over the air at scenes of triumph and tragedy.

'Part of that comes from being very relaxed through his personal characteristics and part through his huge experience after doing it so much. He is very relaxed in front of a microphone. He doesn't have much in the way of inhibitions so there is a minimal part of Murray thinking *how am I coming over?* He just pours it out as it comes and that very, very natural delivery is something that true star commentators uniquely have.

'Another asset Murray had with James or me – and has with Martin – is that, because he's never actually done it, he has a wonderful layman's impression of the glory and magnificence of what's going on. When a racing driver sees somebody win, it's difficult to get truly ecstatic. There is a degree of circumstance about it and it's more of a job. Because Murray hasn't competed as a racing driver he has this romantic view of motor racing, and the years have not diluted it.

'It's easy to look at the back of the field and think *what sort of drivers are those?* but they have worked their way up to be among – arguably – the top 20-odd in the world. If you had Gaston Mazzacane driving you round Silverstone in a road car and he had Schumacher's hat on you'd think *God, this bloke Schumacher's fantastic,* you'd be waxing lyrical about the skill.

'Another thing. I'd go here and there doing the research on fuel loads, new front wings and so on.

> **MURRAY'S MOMENTS**
> Roger Moody, former BBC producer
>
> *Years ago there were four red and white cars, two Alfa Romeos and two Marlboro McLarens. No question: if one of those four crashed Murray would scream "and there you are – the Alfa's gone off! I can't see who it is but I'll let you know in a moment." Whenever he said Alfa it was a McLaren and whenever he said McLaren it was an Alfa.*
>
> *To compound everything he'd say "I think the driver is X" and it would always turn out to be Y. That was just Murray, not because he wasn't paying attention or being unprofessional. He genuinely believed he was making the right identification.*

Murray would always be poking about too, he'd never be one to go and find a quiet restaurant and have a coffee. He'd always be chatting to someone, gathering, gathering – but only to an extent. Because he doesn't have a great technical understanding I used to find that sometimes that played to his advantage. He'd be told things by engineers on the basis that he didn't really understand and therefore they weren't really giving much away. They'd be rather more cautious with someone like me who'd be a lot more analytical. It tickled me: every race he'd pick up a few little gems!'

I remember one of these years the BBC invited various journalists for a mini press conference to announce that, for the forthcoming season, the Walker-Palmer partnership would continue as before. Palmer was relaxed and delighted and recounted a delicious tale of his introduction to the hand waving. Whenever he – Palmer – was talking there was Murray's hand waving *although there was nothing happening*. Palmer laughed as he recounted it, we all laughed and so did Murray: that crackling, gurgling, travelling-at-speed laughter everyone knows so well. If only it had all been like that – but it couldn't be, and it wasn't. In the spring of 1994 Walker and Palmer would be commentating quite normally and, from nowhere, a nightmare engulfed them.

The dignity of two men who never let each other down. Ayrton Senna and Murray Walker at the Autosport awards.

5

TALKING THROUGH A
TRAGEDY

Mark Wilkin sat watching in mounting horror. It was Saturday 30 April, it was 18 minutes into second qualifying for the 1994 San Marino Grand Prix and Roland Ratzenberger's Simtek had just crashed at high speed. Wilkin would produce the BBC's race coverage the following day but, because they weren't covering this qualifying, he could in a sense watch objectively to gauge how *RAI*, the Italian host broadcaster, handled the immediate aftermath of the crash. From this moment on, Imola became a horrific thing testing the limits of language to describe it. This chapter is about how Murray Walker and those around him confronted that. I have quoted them without any adornment at all.

'They had the camera much closer to Roland than they should,' says Wilkin, 'and there were images I can still see and I never want to see again, so we were fairly aware of what they would do if they could. Because of Roland's accident, we sat down that night and discussed at length how we would handle it if we were on the air live. We also talked to John Watson, who was on the air live on *Eurosport*.'

The fact that Ratzenberger died gave Wilkin's concerns an immediacy and a great importance.

'The BBC team had a really serious, in-depth and, as it turned out, prescient conversation about what our policy would be and I had made it clear what we would do. We never imagined it would happen the next day and I said at the time it was unimaginable it could happen to Senna. What we knew was that the *RAI* pictures were going to be as graphic as they could possibly be.

'If you're in the business, as we were, there is a possibility – a serious possibility – that this situation could arise. We used to sit and talk about what we would do *if*. We had various scenarios: what we would do *if* it was the British Grand Prix and the BBC was host broadcaster, what we would do *if* we were at a foreign track where we had no control. Take the Gerhard Berger incident in 1989 [when he crashed at Imola and his Ferrari became a fireball]. *Grandstand* was on the air, they only had the pictures that *RAI* were offering and they went straight back to the snooker. The commentator probably said something like "we'll obviously let you know as soon as we can what's happened to Gerhard and meanwhile here's the snooker."

'At Imola in 1994 we were in a very different position and a more fortunate position than we'd normally have been in, because it was the first time ever we had taken our own live cameras. That meant we were supplementing the Italian coverage with cameras of our own and it gave me, sitting in the control van, an alternative. I could choose to be on their pictures or on mine. My cameras were under my direction but I had a camera in the pit lane and we had also had the benefit, so to speak, of what *RAI* did 24 hours earlier.'

Jonathan Palmer was in the commentary box with Murray – Murray talking – as the Grand Prix got under way. There'd been crashes at the start followed by slow laps under the Safety Car but now Ayrton Senna in a Williams led into the fast Tamburello curve with a wall outside it.

'It happened suddenly,' Palmer says. 'We saw this ricocheting Williams coming off the wall. Initially it looked like it was a big thumping impact. My initial reaction – in the first second or two – wasn't one of *this is critically serious* but within a few more seconds I had this chilly feeling that this really *was* very serious. I remember Senna being still with his head to one side. I remember a little jerk of his head and then stillness. I remember it being a long time before anybody went to him. I remember saying "this is serious, this guy needs help, marshals' help, now."'

'Because of the talk we'd had,' Wilkin says, 'we swiftly moved in to what effectively was a rehearsed sequence. I had no camera at Tamburello but I did have one in the pit lane and Steve Rider was there. He'd never come to a race except the British Grand Prix but, because we were doing an extra half-hour build-up for the first time, we had all these extra people and facilities. Steve – a hugely professional journalist and broadcaster – was a great help to us but in the first instance his job was to go off and get the information. You can't start broadcasting without the information.

'So Murray and Jonathan continued. I firmly believe it was Jonathan's finest hour and Murray was fantastic as well. It was obviously a very difficult time. Murray's natural enthusiasm had to give way to great concern: you slip into the professional routine that we had rehearsed, which was "the medical facilities are absolutely fabulous, the doctors will be on the scene within seconds, everything that can be done will be done." You go into reassuring the viewers. They turn sport on to be entertained, they don't turn it on to see people being killed.'

Palmer remembers 'the sheer ... disbelief. You knew it was happening but it was still unthinkable. This was not just a big motor racing accident, and it was not just somebody getting killed, it was Senna – and it can't happen to Senna. Of all people, how could it be Senna? We'd had our reaction to a fatality – Roland Ratzenberger – and that was yesterday, that was it for the next ten years. Now a huge tidal wave of fact and emotion was coming over.

'Murray was absolutely superb. Through his talents he was, and is, able to express the jubilation and the devastation. The gravitas that he puts into his voice is naturally felt but it is certainly overlaid with a knowledge and responsibility to reflect the mood of what's going on. It's like a switch. Murray goes within seconds from "FANTASTIC! SENNA IS ..." to low-key "difficult situation ... everyone doing the best job they can ... finest doctors ..."'

Wilkin 'cut to the camera which had a wide angle of the pit lane. We didn't immediately go to the Williams garage. We weren't going to do that, we weren't going to intrude on what was clearly a very difficult time for them, so we had general pictures of the crowd and the pit lane. Murray was talking. I switched one of his monitors to the *RAI* output in order that he could see anything that was going on, like an ambulance appearing or the helicopter landing and the medical cars arriving. He effectively continued a radio commentary because we weren't showing those pictures, but he could see them and he was able to say "and now Ayrton Senna has been taken out of the car." We adopted a sombre tone straight away.'

Palmer remembers that 'eventually somebody' – marshals – 'came. Murray picked this up and very soon the scene was helicopters landing and medical people around. I felt at that time that Senna may well be dead. And it went on a long time. Murray set the tone as he would set the tone and the mood on things, and then everyone gets into line behind him. As he picked up the tempo I would as well but you could rely on him to set the tone very accurately.'

Wilkin remembers 'interrupting Murray or waiting until he'd finished and saying "right, now Jonathan – you're a doctor, you know the sort of things they're going to have to do, give us a couple of minutes on that." We knew we were here for a long time. *Grandstand* weren't going to go anywhere else because this was the biggest story of the year. Amongst all of these things Murray had his own personal grief and worry. Senna was a friend of his. The first race of the season, the Brazilian round, we'd spent two or three days with Senna and he had been the most genial, the most kind, the most helpful, the most wonderful host you could possibly hope to meet.

'At Imola, Murray was being the professional broadcaster, the friend, and looking at what this was going to be to motor racing. It was not only the death of Ayrton Senna but possibly the death of motorsport. In many ways Murray handled it better than the rest of us and I never really understood why that was. It may have been because he'd been around motorsport so long he'd seen this before. It wasn't new to him. He was very upset by it but maybe he understood that this happens – none of us had seen it because there hadn't been a death in Grand Prix racing for 12 years. Possibly, too, he was talking and getting it out of himself that way.'

I suggested to Palmer that across the years Murray has had to find a mechanism for coping with tragedies such as Imola.

'I think that's an interesting point. For all of his emotional delivery Murray can be objective and realistic, and be hard about the risks of the sport. He knows that people are going to get killed and that people need to understand there are going to be injuries and fatalities. He's a realist. I think he looks at the rights and wrongs question – should motor racing be happening? – from a pretty cold perspective. If it happens it happens and it's part of motor racing. He will handle it in a professional and dignified way but he certainly wouldn't be the sort ever to go to pieces because of the drama or the tragedy of something. My impression of Murray is that he could be faced with a lot of tragedy around him and he would be deeply reactive at the time but would then move on. He's been around a long time and he's seen an awful lot of tragedy as well as the successes. Life goes on and you get on with the next thing.'

'As I shuffled around, unbeknown to me his
headphone cable got caught around my ankle . . .'

6

THE ECHOES OF ABSENCE

Down all these long years, three men have had to deputise for Murray – Tony Jardine, Simon Taylor and James Allen. In this I do not include Barrie Gill, a noted commentator in his own right before Murray was established as *the* commentator doing every race. Jardine and Taylor deputised because Murray was away doing the British Bike Grand Prix, Allen deputised because he was injured.

To follow Murray was, let us say, a daunting prospect because if you tried to copy him you'd sound absurd and if you didn't try to copy him you'd only emphasise that he was *not* there. Worse, his style and pace – hammered out down all these same long years – had become subliminal. You could turn the volume off and still hear it, loud and clear.

Follow that, as they say, or rather as they did say to Messrs Jardine, Taylor and Allen.

'I first met him when I was tyre fitter/truck driver at the Goodyear Racing Division in 1977,' says Jardine. 'He was friendly to all of us at every level, and we were at the lowest level in the paddock. We were covered in rubber and grime and grease – the monkeys on the poles – and he'd come in under the awning where we were fitting the tyres. He'd got a smile for everybody and he remembered their names. He'd come back a few times and check – "how are those tyres, those qualifiers?" or whatever – and the guys would always help him with the information.

'Murray had clashing events for the BBC and I think Barrie covered in 1984 and had done a few before then. I did 1985 in Germany with James, when Michele Alboreto won. I have to say that it's not just the filling of Murray's boots, it was doing a job which was such a big job that it had me quaking in *my* boots! This wasn't helped by Mr. James Hunt the night before. He was well inebriated. "Come on Teach [Jardine's nickname], let's go out" – he'd found out where the campsite was where all the girlies were staying. He wanted me to go with him, we'd let all the guy ropes down and see what happened! I ended up escaping out of the back door of the restaurant and going upstairs – because each night I was doing homework. You and the rest of the Press

' You can't see Alesi in the Ferrari because it isn't there '

guys were baiting me saying, "oooh, we're down to 48 hours now," then on the morning of it at breakfast "ooooh, in six hours' time ..."'

I must confess that the Press Corps is an extremely brave group except when faced with danger and a goodly portion of this fine body of men were staying in the same hotel as Jardine. The bravery this time was born of the sure knowledge that none of us was going to face The Comparison, or commentating on 27 cars – deceptively difficult to identify under pressure – vanishing over the horizon at immense speed, immediately followed by who knew what? Even without the goading, Jardine was becoming visibly more anxious as these

' ## MURRAY'S MOMENTS
Louise Goodman, ITV's pit lane reporter

He said "now over to Louise Allen" and he said it twice. I made some quip first time around – almost right, Murray or something like that – and the second time he did it I thought he was joking. I thought, right, I'll get you back you bastard and when I "threw" back I said now over to Murray Brundle. At which point all I could hear was laughter going on in my headphones. It was only when he rushed up to me after the race that I realised he hadn't been joking. He came to me absolutely mortified and full of apologies. It didn't bother me. Hell, I'm in esteemed company. '

hours counted down and you could almost lip-read his attempts to memorise the 27: *Patrese – number 22 – green car – Alfa Romeo …*

'The first bit, when Senna went off the line and it all hit me, was like being a rabbit in the headlights. Charlie Balchin was producer and he'd said to me "I don't want you to do what Murray does, I want you to be the antithesis. I don't want you to shout and scream all over the start, just say *they've gone* or whatever. Let it happen."

'When I looked back, I think this was the wrong way. At the green light there were spinning tyres, all the cars setting off – and this gap, this silence in commentary. It didn't work. I came in with "Senna's in the lead" about 10, 12 seconds later. The producer should have said to me to do whatever I felt was right for me. You've got to be your own man. Subsequent to that I was asked to do the Dutch Grand Prix because there was yet another clash but my wife was due to give birth so I couldn't. I think Barrie did it.'

Jardine already understood what following Murray was like. 'I was one of three or four drafted in if he couldn't do a bike race somewhere or a car race at, say, Cadwell Park. In fact I had to do one of his motor cycle events at Cadwell – two races – and I don't know anything about motor cycles. Damon Hill was riding and he was one of the only guys I was familiar with at all. For the two races I was in this control tower and you couldn't see the monitors because the sun was blasting in. I was trying to work out who was who and I was thinking *I don't know how on God's earth Murray does this.* There were 30 riders, I couldn't see it and I was trying to talk over it muddling my way through.

'We crossed over to the powerboats and they'd had two big crashes. Des Lynam said "well, we'll go back to Cadwell Park" so in my ear a voice was saying *we'll do the next race,* which was a Yamaha 350cc one-make race with about 45 of these young madmen in it. This time I knew Damon Hill and about three others.

'Murray would have effort-lessly wallpapered over all the cracks but again I muddled my way through that and came out – no, crawled out – because my brain was absolutely gone. Later I remember speaking to Murray about it and how silly I'd looked. He said "you've got to remember that I was at the motorcycles for about 30 years before I started with the cars! I spent hours and hours walking through the paddock talking to everybody."'

' So Bernie, in the 17 years since you bought McLaren, which of your many achievments do you think was the most memorable? '

This was necessarily hard work and involved considerable memory power but it allowed Murray to arm himself with all manner of information which he could use in his commentaries. As Barrie Gill points out, you'd hear Murray suddenly say 'and here he comes, this 22-year-old son of a Huddersfield butcher who started two years ago ...'

You scarcely noticed this during his commentaries but you certainly noticed when you weren't getting it, as Jardine discovered. As a matter of record, Jardine's commentary at that German Grand Prix was highly competent but I know he will forgive me for saying that wasn't quite the same thing.

' I've just stopped my start watch '

Simon Taylor did a Hungarian Grand Prix in the mid 1980s. 'It was during the James Hunt era, using the same system that the BBC had had to impose – the one microphone because otherwise they weren't able to stop James and Murray interrupting each other. How did I go about it? I simply didn't pretend to be Murray. I just did what I usually do. The important thing to remember is that Murray is completely inimitable and you wouldn't get anywhere pretending to be an understudy to him. All commentators are different. I think any commentator worth his salt develops his own style and does his own thing.'

In December 1995 ITV announced that they had won the contract to cover Grand Prix racing on British television from 1997, something which astonished Britain

– and the BBC who had, after all, broadcast their first live Grand Prix in 1953 and, since 1977, had made the Grand Prix programme something of a national institution.

'The young Ralf Schumacher has been upstaged by the teenager Jenson Button, who is 20'

Murray clearly thought this marked the end of his career because he said that he imagined '1996 is going to be my last season. Everybody is saying "will you go to ITV?" but I don't know if ITV would want me. One point of view would be: "Christ, this old buffer's been doing it ever since God, we want to start with a clean sheet of paper." I would be the last to say that was wrong.'

By the following April strong rumours suggested that ITV wanted Murray to help with the transition from the BBC, something subsequently confirmed.

'From the age of 14 or 15 I listened to Murray Walker and James Hunt and I thought: that's what I want to do.' The speaker is James Allen, journalist, enthusiast and then ITV's man in the pit lane harvesting information and working out race strategies during the races. 'I went out to the United States in 1994 when Nigel Mansell was in IndyCars and in 1995 I wrote Mansell's book with him' [*The People's Champion/*CollinsWillow]. In the States, Allen, a former news editor of *Autosport* magazine, did some television presentation and commentating. Then he came home. 'I knew Murray, but not very well.'

Allen became part of the bid to take the Grands Prix to ITV. 'The thinking was that we should make an entirely new start but here was Murray, willing and available, and he would give it weight and seriousness. You simply could not have taken somebody straight off the street, so to speak – even a very accomplished broadcaster who didn't know about Grand Prix racing – and expect them to be able to do what Murray has done. Grand Prix racing is very complex as well as fast moving.

' MURRAY'S MOMENTS
Martin Brundle, co-commentator

Because of my feet and ankles, it kills me to stand up for a long time and I have to keep shuffling around. That's because of my crash at Dallas in 1984 [his Tyrrell hit a wall in practice]. *At Monza a couple of years ago, as I shuffled round, unbeknown to me his headphone cable got caught around my ankle. As I went for my mid-race reshuffle I had a vision: Murray Walker coming towards me head first, the headphone cable dragging him across the commentary box. He carried on talking as he came towards me looking at me – and I tell you, if looks could kill I would definitely, definitely not be here today.* '

'You add Martin Brundle and you have the perfect contrast, and it's not true that Murray is on an ego trip and wants to have the microphone all the time. He's quite happy to pass the word over to Martin who wants to make some sharp observation. The BBC did not, I think, appreciate quite what a star Murray was. They took him off the shelf for the Grands Prix and put him back on it afterwards. He was on a level with David Jason and stars like that, he really was, and ITV reflected that.

'The BBC rarely covered qualifying and you've to remember that some of the far-away races were only shown as highlights in the middle of the night. ITV have advertised the Grands Prix so that people are aware they're on.'

' Prost can see Mansell in his earphones '

How ITV handled Grand Prix racing – including the fascinating matter of when and why you thread adverts into them, and how for the first time in his life Murray coped with that – will be fully discussed in the chapter 'Commentary box'. I'll content myself here by quoting Keith Mackenzie, who'd been a producer. 'In my days at the BBC I used to do the British Grand Prix and two or three of the foreign ones. I knew Murray very well but I didn't do all 16 or 17 then. When ITV got the contract I left the BBC, went freelance and did all the races with them for the first two years.' In other words, ITV hired

' The Jordan factory is at the factory gates '

people who knew how to do it – led by Murray.

'What you have to remember, and don't let anybody tell you different,' James Allen says, 'is that Murray is a team player who supports members of the team, as well as being a hero. This season [2001] in Australia and Malaysia the local press wanted to interview him because he *is* a hero out there. He has been very supportive of me.'

In 2000 Murray went to the Festival of Speed at Goodwood and broke his hip. The French Grand Prix at Magny-Cours loomed, but of course in a different way to how it had for Jonathan Palmer in 1993. 'I got the phone call on the Tuesday,' Allen says, 'and it said *get your brain together.*'

For Allen, The Comparison would be keener than it ever had been for Gill, Jardine and Taylor. He was, as it seemed, the designated successor because Murray had announced his retirement during 2000 and thus Allen had a whole life to lose. 'I approached it from the point of view that I had to do it in my own way. Murray has made his approach entirely *his* own, it's unique and it will always belong to him. Nobody should ever try to imitate it.

'Commentating on a Grand Prix is a very exciting thing to do and you'll be talking for an hour and a half

but you know that anything can happen at any moment
– it looks like a procession and suddenly a car is on fire.
From everything that is going on, there is a story to tell
in every Grand Prix and that is what Murray has done
so well. After that French Grand Prix he said how well
I'd done ...'

Gill, Jardine, Taylor and Allen are all good men, and
Allen is one of the most perceptive commentators
around. They spoke to you, however, from the bowels
of your television: they didn't burst out of it and were
suddenly across the room speaking to you personally;
and they didn't do it in a voice which might have
stampeded camels. Pardon? We're coming to that when
we've crossed the next sand dune or two in our story.

The trophy was presented by Bernie Ecclestone as a thank-you 'to all our friends at the BBC' when the contract moved to ITV.

7

I THINK YOU'LL FIND

The Walker-Hunt duet seemed more alchemy than chemistry: one of those rare things where two completely different strengths complement each other perfectly. Nobody, I am sure, ever suspected a comparable duet could ever be constructed. Remarkably, it has been. Martin Brundle has achieved that with Murray and since he is as capable of commentating on his own situation as on anything else, here he is.

'I knew Murray reasonably well before I started working with him because over the years he'd been a commentator when I was a driver, but not such that I would speak to him between races or spend a lot of social time with him or anything like that. Back in those days the BBC didn't have any extra programmes so he hadn't actually interviewed me that many times. I think I can remember just about every one of the interviews I had with him as a driver. The BBC didn't have the budget or the air time to do the sort of lifestyle stuff that is done now. And let's be honest, Grand Prix racing wasn't so high profile, was it? So I knew him professionally, I didn't know him particularly well personally. He'd always been a supporter of mine, he'd always looked after me through the good times and the bad times.'

How did you approach partnering him? You're going to have this man standing beside you shouting all round the world.

'I didn't really want to do the TV at that stage because I wanted to remain a Grand Prix driver. At the same time I realised that getting in at the beginning of the ITV Formula 1 coverage wasn't something to be thrown away lightly. I really wanted to carry on driving but equally if I didn't take it somebody else would and I might never get the offer again. When I did reluctantly sign up I sat down and thought about it and how I wanted to approach it. I remember we were doing a press launch at Gray's Inn Road, where ITV and ITN are, and I had dinner with Murray the night before because I wanted to work with him. I felt that was very important: to work *with* him, and I came at it from the point of view that I was moving into his territory. I wanted to do what I needed to do but in a way where I could work with him on air. It was quite a lot different for him as well, BBC to ITV, and I wanted to make a team out of it as much as anything else.

'I think it was a smart move – and the smartest thing I ever did was right from the beginning I thought: well, he stands up so I'll stand up. I wanted to communicate with him *and* with the viewers so that they became part of our conversation. I didn't just want to do my bit when he wasn't doing his bit. I think that was important to him and it was certainly important to me, and I think that's why we gelled – because we do work together and not just play different roles.'

Everybody who has worked with him has had to face the fact that he makes mistakes. Do you correct them or let them go?

'We both make mistakes and let's be very clear on that, it's not exclusive to Murray. He does make mistakes, of course, and I do scoop them up as gently as I can. Some of them I don't bother with, some I will where I think it's fundamentally important to the

' MURRAY'S MOMENTS
Tony Jardine, ITV broadcaster and PR man

It was the BBC's Grandstand *programme on a Bank holiday, with Des Lynam hosting the coverage which moved around various events and Murray at a track somewhere. Unaware that Lynam had switched back to him, he was conducting a private conversation with himself, blasphemies and all. CHRIST!!! ... LOOK AT THAT ... CHRIST!!! And the nation got the lot.* '

viewers' understanding of the race, and sometimes I have a bit of a general laugh about it. I think we both use humour quite well in what we do. We both like to get a bit of that in and it is a very useful communications tool as long as you hold the balance between that humour and being serious.'

When Brundle has corrected him he has done so with affectionate decorum, murmuring 'I think you'll find, Murray' so diplomatically that viewers in the Foreign Office must find themselves murmuring in approval.

'I have a lot of respect for Murray. He's been doing that longer than I've been alive, he's forgotten more than I will ever know. Of course I have specific knowledge of driving the cars and so on, and I can read that aspect of it – that's why I'm in the commentary box. You've got to leave your ego out of the box. He is a professional broadcaster and I'm a racing driver and we do different jobs. It is my job to know what's going to happen next and to put the viewers behind the wheel.

'The great thing about commentating with Murray is that if I am trying to work something out I can stop talking in the certain knowledge that he can start talking. He can always say something, always. Therefore, when I'm trying to get my head round something – for example the teams don't always know their own strategies, they change them, they react to the race – we are trying to second guess what they're trying to do or what they might do now, given the circumstances.

'The fact is that Murray is such a professional, he is the continuity man, he's the colour commentator. It's his job to say what's happening, my job to say why and, I hope, it works beautifully. You wouldn't expect him to know all the technical stuff any more than you'd expect me to be doing the race commentary, and that's why they throw to Murray. He always does the start, he always does the podium procedure: we've got territory. If there's a big move coming up it's mine. That's almost an unwritten rule, because his job is "the sky's blue, Schumacher looks like he's going to win" and my job is to say "the effect of the sky being blue on the cars is *this*" and "the reason why Schumacher is going to win is *this*."

'And we have had five races so far this year – Brazil, Argentina, Imola, Schumacher and Monaco'

'Our relationship has developed, because in the first year – first couple of years, really – we had to sit down two or three times and sort a few things out. We were talking over each other and all that. We have two microphones and sometimes it feels like we've got three because we've got so much to say and we both want to say it at the same time! That's because we are both so enthusiastic about it, we absolutely are.

'It's a crying shame it's coming to an end because I think this year [2001] it is just spot on. It feels seamless. There's no competition between us, we're both confident enough about what we're doing and where we're going to help each other along. And we are enjoying ourselves.

'People invite you into their lounges, don't they? They're going to give up their free time to watch their chosen sport and they don't want aggression coming at them through a corner of their lounge, they want information and entertainment, they want knowledge and they want to enjoy what they are watching. The one thing I completely underestimated is how seriously people take their sports commentaries. They really do.'

' As you can see, visually, with your eyes '

A couple of times Brundle was competing at the 24-hour race at Le Mans, which clashed with the Canadian Grand Prix, and Mark Blundell (already over there driving for PacWest in IndyCars) deputised.

Blundell describes Murray as 'an institution. It's remarkable that he's done what he has and he's still doing what he's doing. He's still as sharp as can be and on the ball, does all his research and he's absolutely great. I found it easy with him. You like him, you know who he is, you respect him and there is no other voice for Formula 1 in Britain and everywhere else they take the programme. It's an honour and a pleasure to work alongside him and he makes it incredibly easy. Now and again he has his fluffs but that's Murray. I'm sure that half the people you talk to enjoy that side of it.'

I put to Blundell the point I had put to Brundle. You have to decide how to cope with the fluffs.

'That's OK because it's Murray. You know that it's going to come, you know at some point it's going to happen. There is no way that you are going to sit there for two hours of Grands Prix and there won't be a fluff. It's odds on. That's loveable – there's no down side to it. You wouldn't be harsh over it because there's no point. You have already absorbed the information and you've had time to think about it. You didn't have to commit yourself and he did, and it's a lot harder than people think. It really is.'

. . . and James would be asleep.

8

BEST OF BOTH WORLDS

The voice which travels across your living room does not just do so in Newcastle upon Tyne but Newcastle in Ontario and Newcastle, New Brunswick; Newcastle in New South Wales, and Newcastle, Natal. I wish I could add Newcastle, New Zealand, but there isn't one there and, in the considered opinion of motorsport journalist Eoin Young, a New Zealander, the Kiwi population may not necessarily want the Murray treatment anyway.

This is something of a paradox because in Australia Murray is all the clichés you could wish for, from icon to institution to folk hero. Barrie Gill remembers 'once he was going to Australia with James Hunt. When they landed there was this huge crowd waiting and James Hunt thought it was for him – and it was the Murray Walker Fan Club. They all had the tee-shirts on. Murray didn't know how to take it until he realised.'

Stuart Sykes works for the Australian Grand Prix. 'Ever since Murray's first visit for the 1985 race in Adelaide he has attracted an enormous personal following. This year [2001] he and his wife Elizabeth were special guests at the official Grand Prix Ball on the Friday evening, where he was moved to tears by the speeches and by an award which was a replica of the very handsome, steering-wheel-based trophy given to the Australian Grand Prix winner.

'On the Sunday morning we kept a surprise for him – an invitation to join the drivers' parade before the race. It meant Murray had to walk the length of the pit lane, opposite the main grandstand, both before and after the parade lap. As we waited to go out to the car, some of the most hard-bitten of the marshals came up to him for autographs and almost all of them were saying "Mr. Walker" as a mark of respect. 'As I escorted him to the car – and back again – I can tell you that the reception was quite extraordinary. It went far beyond the cheers and waves any of the drivers received. As he went to leave the pit lane at the end he turned and gave a farewell bow. You should have heard the noise.

' *And now the boot is on the other Schumacher* '

'Two weeks later I was working at the Malaysian Grand Prix and Murray confessed that he hoped there would be no repeat of the reception he had been given in Oz – there was simply no time to get his work done properly!'

Before we leave the Grand Prix Ball, Linda Pattisson says 'it's easy to miss the depth of the guy. There is this modesty about him. He's still amazed that things come to him. The Grand Prix Ball in Australia was dedicated to him, they invited Elizabeth to go out with him and again there was this amazement it happened. "Guess what?" he'd say.'

Moving about in Australia is, evidently, as difficult for him as it is in Britain. 'If you ever walk around with Murray trying to get from *A* to *B* it's impossible,' Keith Mackenzie says. 'You get stopped all the time – they want autographs and they want to speak to him. I can remember walking down the main street in Melbourne when we'd gone off for a bite to eat or to do a bit of shopping and you couldn't because everyone wanted to pat him on the back and say hello. Incredible!'

'Nigel Mansell had a problem with the wheel-nut on his Williams, then he went on to win brilliantly for Ferrari!'

This makes Eoin Young's assertion all the more surprising. 'In Australia I always hear that everybody is a great fan of his but in New Zealand – and I don't know if it's just the people I know out there – they are always very vociferous and say "oh, he misses things."

They say it as though they *mean* it. New Zealand has got a lot of the tall poppy [syndrome]' – an irreverence towards those who get to the top. 'Take Denny Hulme. He was World Champion in 1967 and he never got into the Hall of Fame in New Zealand.

'In Australia Murray brings tears to their eyes and in New Zealand they wish somebody else was doing it! I like him and I have always stood up for him because from the first days I was watching it I knew he was doing it off a little monitor in a horrible little wardrobe and half the time he couldn't see the cars.'

' . . . and he's lost both right front tyres'

Young outlines his admiration with an anecdote. He went to see a race in the second season of the British Touring Car Championship and 'it was boring as hell. I met Dick Bennetts [Kiwi and team owner] and he asked what I thought of it? I repeated: boring as hell. "Ah," he said, "missed the Murray factor, did you?" That was a measure of how Murray could transform an event where nothing was happening. He'd have had people running to the television ...'

The Canadians are, by nature, much more restrained than all this. 'Canada has been taking coverage since the BBC started covering it,' Gerry Donaldson says. 'We got it from day one. Murray's got a huge following and he's highly regarded – it's the same as in Britain. People find his mistakes aggravating but mostly endearing. It's part of his *schtick* – an American Yiddish word, I think. It means his act, what he is known for as a personality.

'Yes, he does sound a terribly British voice but is admired for the same reason that James Hunt was greatly admired. We are dealing with a colony, after all! Murray's voice is indelibly associated with the sport, as was James and now Martin Brundle. I think he has a bigger following in Australia: Canadians are a little less demonstrative but he is equally liked there. If he walked down a street in Montreal he'd certainly be recognised. As Jacques Villeneuve points out, Canadian fans are better behaved and less likely to mob people. I've seen Murray surrounded by autograph hunters, though, having friendly chats with them.'

'Andrea de Cesaris, who has won more Grands Prix than anyone else without actually winning one of them . . .'

Andrew Embleton, a devoted motorsport follower in South Africa, says 'we have had Murray Walker for as long as we have had Grands Prix on television and that certainly goes back to the early 1980s. We have our own continuity chaps who do the introduction and try to give some local flavour but as soon as the race is due to start our television station switches to the UK.

'I think he has been well respected as a knowledge-able commentator and people have grown to enjoy his "bloops" as things to be expected from him. We love the "Barrichello's just spun off" from Murray followed by a quiet "... I think it was Schumacher, Murray" from MB. Certainly Murray brought motor racing to the far-flung areas, to people who have never been near a Formula 1 car nor are ever likely to do so. His enthusiasm is always enough to make a dull race come alive although as non-partisan watchers we sometimes felt his support of British drivers was very obvious – but then he is British!'

' I didn't see the time, largely because there wasn't one '

What seems (slightly) surprising is that these countries, so anxious to stress their nationhood in so many ways, are still happy to take the voice of the mother country in at least *this*. To which Donaldson, a respected Canadian journalist, says 'coverage is carried by the TSN network and I am involved in the pre-race show giving a Canadian point of view with a studio anchor guy who is Canadian. On the parade lap we shut up and turn over to Murray and Martin. Then we also do a post-race bit.' The Canadians are getting the best of both worlds: old and new.

Or, as Barrie Gill puts it, 'Murray Walker is as well known in Canada as he is in South Africa as he is in Australia as he is in New Zealand as he is in Hong Kong. I was in Dubai last week and a bloke was asking me how Murray Walker was.'

The full reach of Murray's commentary is: Saudi Arabia, Yemen, Oman, UAE, Qatar, Bahrain, Iraq, Iran, Kuwait, Syria, Lebanon, Jordan, Palestine, Egypt, Sudan, Libya, Tunisia, Algeria and Morocco (Arab Radio & Television); Australia (Nine Network), Malaysia (TV3), Canada (TSN), New Zealand (TVNZ) and South Africa (SABC).

All of which makes me wonder how many camels, resting in the shade, have been rudely woken by a voice from a television in a nearby dry-mud hut.

'There's one red light on ... two ... three, four ... five and ... in a moment ... it will be ... GO! GO! GO!'

And have risen, and gone.

'Murray started rocking, so I started rocking with him. We must have looked like a pair of windscreen wipers.'

9

COMMENTARY
BOX

It's easy to forget that the old days weren't very long ago and how complete a change the technology has brought. Once upon a time – only just over 20 years ago – the coverage of Formula 1 was not remotely as it is now. Roger Moody explains that when the BBC 'went back into motor racing we never went live, there were only highlights on a Sunday night. Murray would go out to the circuits on a Thursday and stay for the Friday and Saturday practices, then leave and come back to the studios where I, as the assistant producer, would take the incoming feed of the race and edit it down to an hour's programme. We would dub it, put the words on and I think it was only Murray in those days. It would go out as a highlights show.

'I remember one occasion when Murray had started his commentary and there was some sort of foul-up. We played the tape again, cued Murray and finished the whole thing. It was several minutes to transmission, which was cutting it quite fine. We yelled down to the guys in videotape, *get the tape back on cue and stand by for transmission to run it in live*. The videotape editor had gone back to the original start. Off we went and after about three minutes you suddenly heard Murray saying "I think I'll have to do that again" – which you can't do commentating on a live race. The whole thing fell off the air, most unusual for the BBC. We had an on-screen caption saying *We apologise …*'

This is an aeon away from today's wall-to-wall coverage and thereby hangs a tale because, even when the *Grand Prix* programme moved forward to covering the races live, James Hunt had a clause in his contract allowing him to physically miss a race of his choice per season. He generally chose Austria. Murray arrived at

MURRAY'S MOMENTS
Keke Rosberg, 1982 World Champion

[As related by Murray himself, discussing the Curse of Walker whereby as soon as he focused on a race leader that driver's luck seemed to change disastrously]: *In 1982 Rosberg came up to Murray and Murray said 'you're doing well in the championship.' Rosberg said 'yes, and if I'm leading a race do you mind not mentioning it …'*

the Österreichring resembling a hunter-gatherer, hunted and gathered, and departed after Saturday qualifying for London where, on the Sunday, he and Hunt commentated as if they were at the circuit. During the commentary Murray artfully inserted a phrase like 'as Ron Dennis told me outside the McLaren motorhome yesterday' which (if you knew) sounded like code for 'well, I *was* there.' He wasn't, I suspect, at all pleased to be absent from even this one race.

Mark Wilkin explains that 'we used to try and control Murray. Commentary is a bit like a runaway truck and as a producer you are standing with your foot on the brake. Sometimes the truck has taken over and you're flying down the hill out of control, other times you've got it and you're nudging it. I think as a producer you can't grab the steering wheel and turn it 90 degrees, but you can get control again. The way to do that with Murray was to find a pause when he finally got to the end of the sentence. Then you'd say "right, Murray, listen to me" and when he was listening to you he couldn't be speaking at the same time. You'd use that to slow him down and then ask him to do the top six runners in the race at that moment.

'One of his problems was that he'd look at the timing monitor and not at the screen so as he was reading the top six a guy down here's had a crash and burst into flames. That's because Murray hasn't got two pairs of eyes. That's the producer's job: to warn, to tell, to explain. He took it very well.

'Murray is up there with all the great commentators. He is up there because anyone who achieves the 'voice of' status on BBC television is clearly huge and it doesn't matter then whether they have great technical insights, great knowledge of the sport or whatever. They are imparting their enthusiasm and knowledge in an entertaining and interesting way. And that clearly Murray did.'

Keith Mackenzie straddled the transition of Formula 1 coverage from BBC to ITV. In general, he says, 'it's probably one of the most difficult sports in the world to cover and I say that from Murray's point in the commentary box all the way to anybody that's directing a race or involved in it. For a start it's going at 170 to 180 miles an hour, and it's not predictable. I used to do the Grand National and the difference between that at 40 miles an hour and Formula 1 at nearly 200 is colossal – and of course there's more than one race going on [drivers attacking and defending all round the circuit]. Murray in a commentary box doesn't have a much better view of anything than somebody at home watching it on television. The only thing he's got is timing screens, but when you're flicking through timing screens your eyes are taken off the monitor, and that's where the race is happening.

'Often when a viewer at home sees something and Murray doesn't react for four or five seconds, it's probably because he's flicking through the timing screens. Then somebody shouts in his ear and says, *hey, so and so's happened* and all of a sudden he does the commentary as if it's just happened and the viewer says to himself *hey, that happened five seconds ago.*

'Did I ever have to restrain him? Restrain is probably not the right term. Basically we are in Murray's ear all the time and there are two aspects to this. If we are the host broadcaster [the British Grand Prix] and I am directing the race, then obviously I am helping him because I'm telling him what I'm going to do or if I'm going to put a replay on, so he's wise to what's coming up. When he's overseas he doesn't have any producer's talk-back from the person who is directing the race and therefore he doesn't have any idea what's coming up. He gets no clue as to whether the coverage is going to go from the leader down to fifth or whether there's going to be a replay of this or that.

' *Only a few laps to go and then the action will begin, unless this is the action which it is* '

'At Silverstone, however, I can actually talk to him. If I cut to a spin I can tell him who's spun so he doesn't have to think about it, doesn't have to look and say *who is that?* That means he gets a bit of extra help but at a foreign Grand Prix he doesn't get any help at all, he's really commentating off the pictures.

'We are sitting in the truck and we have eyes on everything. We are helping him by telling him what we spot and we've also intelligence down in the pits [James Allen and Louise Goodman] so we know something about pit stops and that sort of thing, but the main direction he gets from us during the race is to have the occasional pause: "take a breath, do a 1 to 10 or a 1 to 6."

'He is juggling a lot of things in his mind at any given moment. He stands up, which is very unusual for a sports commentator and it means anybody that works with him has to stand up. He's got bits of paper and notes and facts and figures stuck all round the wall and all round the window in his eye line. *Plus* he's got three or four monitors up there: what ITV are sending, *plus* the world feed which is a continuous feed of the race, *plus* a couple of timing monitors. He's a lot to look at. Rather than sitting at home having one screen and being able to see everything that's going on, he's flicking his eyes from one screen to another. *Plus* on the timing screens you have a number of different pages so he's having to flick buttons to look from page 1 to page 4 to page 3 and so on. *Plus* most commentary boxes – not all – have some sort of view of the pit lane and the main straight so he's able to glance out of the window and have a general look to see what's going on.

'Commentating, however, is very much off the monitor with as much help as we can give him. I think it's fantastic that you virtually wind him up, switch him on and away he goes for an hour and a half.

'The interesting thing was that when ITV took over, the facilities – in other words the outside broadcast technical people and equipment – were BBC because BBC Outside Broadcasts are a facility company and can work for anybody. The last Silverstone Grand Prix I did for the BBC was with BBC equipment and crews, and the following year when I did my first ITV British Grand Prix I virtually had the same vehicles, the same equipment and the same crews – so from that point of view it was a very smooth change over. In a similar way, there were a lot of people who'd worked on *Grand Prix* with Murray and a number of those people moved across to work with ITV – so again there were a lot of familiar faces and people who knew what they were doing.

'... with Alesi in 4th and 5th ...'

'Obviously we sat down and had various meetings and discussions about how the hell we were going to handle the commercial breaks. We knew we were up against it because nobody in the UK had ever watched Formula 1 with commercial breaks but it was one of those things that we could do nothing about. Should we go for race coverage running at a two-minute delay? If we did, we'd always be wise: we'd take a break because we'd know nothing's happened in the last two minutes. We decided not to do that – it wasn't right because it wouldn't be live. Should we try and push the picture 'back' somehow and get advertisers that would put up with having part of the Grand Prix still running in a corner? We decided against that.

'Then we went through how many breaks should we have. We knew how much commercial content they wanted but should we have two-minute breaks, three-minute breaks, one-minute breaks? The decision

❛ MURRAY'S MOMENTS
Mark Blundell, driver and sometime commentator

> I've done commentaries with Murray when Martin Brundle has been at Le Mans. I did Canada a couple of years. I rolled up, five minutes to go and got in the commentary box. Murray was already there. He started doing all these breathing exercises. Next thing he's standing up, I'm sitting down and I wondered when he *was going to sit down. He never did.*
>
> I felt relaxed but out of place so I thought I'll stand up with him. *I stood. All of a sudden he started rocking – that's how he does it: he's talking, he's so* into *it that he's got a rhythm from side to side, so I* started rocking with him. We must have looked like a pair of windscreen wipers. ❜

was we'd always have five commercial breaks during the race of 2 minutes and 10 seconds each – only 2 minutes 10s, but believe me they are the longest 2 minutes 10!'

They must watch helplessly hoping that *nothing* happens although 'during that, of course, Murray and Martin's commentary continues because it goes to the rest of the world, not just to ITV. Once ITV are clear and into the break we re-cue Murray and Martin and they do a two-minute commentary until we ask them to be quiet again ready for ITV to rejoin. Then they'll recap on anything relevant that the ITV audience missed.

'It's done fairly carefully, and during the two minutes we try and discourage them from getting involved in anything important because we want that on ITV. We don't want it thrown away during the two minutes that they're not on. That's another pressure for Murray on top of all the other pressures. The biggest problem any commentator has is referring back. If you know you are live for an hour you can refer back to anything in that hour, but when you've had a number of two-minute commercial breaks you might just say "well, as you saw earlier on" and in fact the viewer might not have done. You have to remember not to do that.

'If it's really serious and we've missed it during a break, usually some kind journalist will mention it in the press on the Monday morning *as if we knew it was going to happen*. We take every possible piece of intelligence and we never take a break without seriously thinking about where we should take it, particularly with pit stops and overtaking moves, but a lot of people fail to realise that. They think we almost take the breaks and miss things on purpose! They think we're stupid because we took a break when something was about to happen – if we had a crystal ball it would be wonderful.

'During the Friday and the Saturday practice sessions before our very first Grand Prix, in Australia, we rehearsed quite a lot because the one thing that Murray had never done – well, *we'd* never done, really – was this: if there was an incident while we were away on a commercial break we obviously had to run it in. That incident could be even ten seconds before the end of the break. Murray and Martin had to discipline themselves to welcome the viewers back and then recap on something which we would run in ourselves over the top of whatever was happening with the coverage. They needed to talk about that and then, of course, we'd go back live. Murray coped fine, because coming out of a break and saying we'd missed something is only really like the host broadcaster running a replay of something you haven't seen live.'

Murray, however might be in full flow, or more accurately the words might be flowing out of him in a mighty torrent. He has to be halted in his tracks for the break and he had not faced that before in the whole of his professional career.

'We give him a bit of warning that a commercial break is coming up. We'll say "we're looking for a break," then we decide we will and we say "OK, take us to a break." All we say is "lead to a break, Murray" and after moving into it – just to make sure he's stopped talking – I push a button and say "right, no more commentary." And we roll the break. The first year we tried not to do that because we didn't want to signpost the breaks too much but the second and subsequent years we decided to be slightly more 'honest' as far as the commentary went and Murray would say "we're leaving Magny-Cours for a couple of minutes and then we'll be back."

'If I was Michael Schumacher, which of course I'm not'

'The breaks are fluid. We make the final decision in the truck but we take as much advice as we can. We often say to Martin "we are thinking of taking a break, d'you think that's a good idea?" He'll say "I'd just hang on another lap" or "OK, it looks pretty good." We ask the guys in the pits if there is any likelihood of any pit stops coming up, can they see any activity. They'll say "it's all quiet." Obviously before the race we've found out when the pit stops are likely to happen so we've an idea when the first stops might be, say, lap 20 or maybe between laps 20 and 26. We've a lot of information and anything we have learned we pass on to Murray. He is so experienced and so adaptable, and once you get into the flow of doing it you just do it. I have never known him lose his cool, never ever. He just seems to cope with everything.'

' And there's the man in the green flag '

Louise Goodman has a roving commission. 'I'm basically working on my own and I call them and tell them what's going on. I'll say "OK, now I'm outside Ferrari. I'll let you know when Schumacher's with me." Then I'll say "come to me now." Someone holds out a board in front of Murray and Martin that says *Louise* and they go straight down to me – they might not even know what I've got.'

Simon Taylor puts today's television coverage into perspective. 'The point is, and this is something that has changed radically over the last 20 years, the television audience is enormous and isn't necessarily motor racing-expert. The vast majority who follow it closely and enjoy it hugely have never been to a motor race and never will go. They are people who have come to Formula 1 via television and within that you can understand the shift of emphasis which has followed ITV taking over from the BBC. ITV are in the business of expanding their audience for very good and sensible commercial reasons and they know that what they put on from a Grand Prix weekend has to be entertainment.

This is where Murray's supreme ability comes into play because he is an entertainer.

'In a way, Murray never set out to be an entertainer and it's almost unconscious. It's not actually unconscious because he's too skilful a broadcaster and he knows exactly what he's doing. Murray's prime quality, the major ingredient of his commentaries, is his enthusiasm. That enthusiasm is totally, totally genuine. It is not something that anybody could ever simulate. If Murray had lost – at any time over the last half century – any of his enthusiasm then instantly the Murray magic would have disappeared. But it hasn't disappeared because his enthusiasm now is absolutely as strong as ever it was. It is that enthusiasm which is so infectious and able to communicate itself to people sitting on their sofas: people who have never seen a Formula 1 car with their own eyes, never been to a Grand Prix. Yet they can *feel* the excitement because Murray communicates that.'

'*The flying Finn in front from Scotland . . .*'

The testament to the Walker-Brundle duet is that it's so professional you can't tell all this is going on. The coverage is very modern in tone and outlook, and that is further testament because a man within sight of 80 is the pillar – a youthful pillar. The old days might not have been long ago but the old 'un himself was always right here and now.

'I'm never having bloody red roast beef with you again Murray!'

10

GAFFES FROM THE GAFFER

M urray Walker does not necessarily accept that he makes gaffes, only prophesies which in some mystifying way fail to come true. Others don't quite see it like this but, whatever you want to call them, the prophesies have had a curious by-product – long ago they became a central part of his appeal. There are pages of them on the Internet, as if some curious sect was spreading a gospel about their leader; and of course, once his reputation for thundering blunders was established, each new one fed that. The inconvenient fact that he didn't make many was obscured. There are (of course) no web pages charting the thousands upon thousands of gaffe-free words he has spoken, most of them dug from the heat of battle.

In keeping with his philosophy of openness and honesty, he freely discusses them and when I interviewed him in 1982 said his favourite was an off-road saloon car race when he proclaimed 'the advantage of being the leader is that you have a clear windscreen', and *as* he had spoken these words the car, a BMW, plunged into banking. (My own favourites are the exchange with Ecclestone about buying/not buying McLaren and, in the pit lane at Silverstone, preparing to go out in a Formula 1 car, stalling it *violently,* grinning hugely and shouting 'I've done it again!' The second is not even a verbal blunder, more a literal knee-jerk, but the whole mood of it captures the man.)

Murray does after-dinner speeches based on his mistakes. The gaffes, says Linda Pattisson, are 'because Murray's verbals are so much more than anybody else's and motor racing is so unpredictable, but that became the affection that everybody had. At the after dinner speeches it was what people expected him to tell about, and that's the amusing part – it's what people want to hear about. Because he has a gentle affection for himself, and is quite happy to take the Mickey, those are the things that he will come out with. However, I have heard him put the record straight and say "that one wasn't mine" or "it was taken out of context." Within the speech he will normally bring in a few of those to prove he's not all about mistakes. He'd talk about when he hit Nigel Mansell on the head – most people had seen that on the telly, anyway. He does have a brilliant memory and he remembers all those things.'

Indeed most people would probably remember approaching Mansell, who had a bump on the head, and tapping it with a microphone, but leaving that aside, there is a context here too. Roger Moody was the producer and he had hustled Murray from the commentary box to scour for interviews before everyone vanished (as they do after races). Moody is sure the celebrated tap only happened 'because he'd just come across in haste.'

Mansell took the tap in good part – this same Mansell who Murray would describe as 'one of the thinnest-skinned, easily offended, prickly people I have

‘
MURRAY'S MOMENTS

Barrie Gill, former commentator

Murray and I were to do a commercial together and the script played to the fact that there were two of us. I asked "could we be in separate boxes?" because standing next to him you pick up his inflections.

I used to do the German Grand Prix every time Murray was doing the motor bikes [each summer Murray commentated on the British Bike Grand Prix]. *Jonathan Martin would say "just remember Barrie, you're not Murray. You don't have to keep shouting. This sport has its own energy – you don't have to create the energy. Just let it happen." No-one can get excited the way Murray can get excited.*

’

ever met in my life,' adding that it was just this which made him such a magnificent driver ('balls like melons') and 'you probably can't have one without the other.'

Yes, life with Our Nige was rarely a symphony of harmonies and Roger Moody recounts a story about that, wherein however Mansell was the innocent party. 'The first Mexican Grand Prix of the modern age was in 1986 and we all went out for that – Mansell was going for the championship. We'd found in Zona Rosa, in central Mexico City, not a red light area but restaurants and shops! We'd found a very nice roast beef restaurant, and Murray likes his roast beef. This was the Friday, we were all there and it was Murray's birthday. A journalist had told Nigel and Murray was absolutely thrilled that Mansell had taken the time out to come and eat with him.'

' You might not think that's cricket, and it's not, it's motor racing '

Mansell: 'What are you eating, Murray?'

Walker: 'I'm having beef.'

Mansell: 'Don't think I'll have that, it might play up.'

Walker: 'No, no, go on, it'll be all right.'

'So,' Moody says, 'Mansell had a slice of red roast beef off the trolley and we had a good evening. Next day during practice I have never seen anyone get round that track quicker, then out of the car and running like a stag. He did that about seven times. At the end of the race he came up to Murray and me and said "I'm never going to have bloody red roast beef with you again."

'Nigel was always a great foil for Murray. He had a lot of time for him. Like a lot of us he thought Nigel moaned a bit, but that's Nigel. And Nigel was bloody good journalistic fodder, wasn't he?'

He was.

Mark Wilkin makes a more serious point, or rather several. 'There are lots of people who said in my time that he made mistakes, that he predicted things which were instantly proved to be wrong, that he often didn't leave himself room to get out of things and that he'd go flying off down what turned out to be a blind alley and have no way back – but it was half the entertainment. You'd find he didn't finish half the sentences because something else overtook him. That was something we talked about a lot: how to do commentary, what are you trying to say, how are you trying to say it. What happens when you see a car spinning off and you don't know which one it is? You might know it's a Ligier but you wouldn't know which so rather than say "it's Martin Brundle, it's Martin Brundle" let's say "it's definitely a Ligier" – and wait.

' The atmosphere is so tense you could cut it with a cricket stump '

'We'd all be sitting there. We'd have a lap-charter in the commentary box, a producer, the expert commentator – and latterly a producer in a van – and we'd all try to work out who it was. We felt it was wrong to take a guess which turned out to be wrong. As soon as Murray went for an identification, it worked like this: one of us would point to who it was, or I'd tell him in his ear, or he'd just go for it. If he was right we'd all put our thumbs up. It was a team effort and he was very much aware that it was a team effort.

' MURRAY'S MOMENTS
Roger Moody, former BBC producer

It was the French Grand Prix down in Dijon, and the French didn't usually come up with very good commentary boxes. We were out in the open with straw matting above us and the heavens opened up. The water poured off the matting all over the monitors and they blanked out.

Murray was saying "well, I haven't got any pictures here but I assume you have back in London so I'll just keep on talking about what I can't see." I was rushing around trying to find an engineer who could help and the only one I could find had been enjoying the French wine and was slumped against the back of the outside broadcast truck.

You've the matting, the water coming through, blank screens – and he's still talking. It's all part of the Murray Walker folklore. And he coped. I honestly don't recall any time that Murray couldn't cope with … anything. '

Mark Blundell (with Johnny Herbert) who found himself moving in the commentary box alongside Murray like windscreen wipers – see page 124! (Formula One Pictures)

When the pain had gone. (LAT)

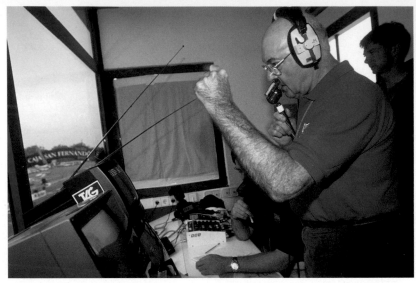

Formula 1 is one of the most difficult sports in the world to cover. (Sporting Pictures UK Ltd)

This is the sort of view he used to get. (Formula One Pictures)

Mansell vindicates his struggle and his life in Hungary as he crosses the line to take the 1992 title. At this moment Murray was baying 'Mansell finishes … and he's World Champion!' before immediately handing to Hunt who said 'and a tremendous effort from Nigel Mansell. He's fought long and hard for this.' (LAT)

Mansell explaining how it felt. (Formula One Pictures)

Murray has a lump in his throat as Damon Hill wins the 1996 World Championship in Japan. (LAT)

You can talk about it, Murray, but this is how you do it. (Sporting Pictures UK Ltd)

The voice was as familiar in Australia as Britain – and familiar in many other places, too. Melbourne pays homage and says farewell. (Sporting Pictures UK Ltd)

Back in the turret after half a century. Murray and Sherman tank at the Tank Museum, Bovington, in 2001. (Roland Groom, courtesy of the museum)

Above, left: *The passion of man for machine – especially this man and this machine.* (LAT)

Left: *Thanks! Murray receives a 'Bernie' for outstanding services from the man himself in Spain, 2001.* (Sporting Pictures UK Ltd)

Below, left: *Silverstone, July, 2001.* (Sporting Pictures UK Ltd)

Above and right. *The gala farewell at London's Café Royal. Motorsport says goodbye to Murray Walker and Murray says goodbye to them.* (LAT)

Above: … *the boot was on the other Schumacher. Indianapolis, 2001 – Murray's last race as an ITV commentator.* (Sporting Pictures UK)

Below, left: *Never short of a few thousand words.* (Orange)

Below, right: *In the end, all the world was a stage for Murray Walker. With Sir Jackie Stewart at the 2002 BAFTA awards.*

'I remember Derek Warwick's crash at Monza [on the first lap of the 1990 Italian Grand Prix]. As soon as that happened I said "it's Derek." Murray knew that if I said something it was because I knew it was right and I wasn't guessing. Murray immediately went with "it's Derek Warwick."'

Simon Taylor, himself an extremely experienced commentator, has a serious point of his own. 'I don't think Murray ever makes a mistake through ignorance. He makes a mistake through excitement, perhaps, and that is an endearing quality. If you go to any Grand Prix in any country in the world, however major the time change – you may be in the rain in Japan or whatever – Murray is already there going round the paddock, and when Murray goes round the paddock he doesn't just talk to the drivers, he talks to the team personnel, the engineers and the mechanics. Because Murray is such a nice man everybody is delighted to talk to him. His huge knowledge and understanding of Formula 1, which informs his commentaries, comes from the fact that he is known and liked and accepted and trusted. He doesn't betray a confidence. And he does his homework.'

Murray questions whether the BMW-windscreen-banking debacle was a mistake at all. 'Yes, it is a mistake because what I said wasn't true – but it is a failure by force of circumstances to co-ordinate your words with the action. I don't regard that as a culpable error: it's an amusing mistake. Now if I was making genuine mistakes on account of the fact that I hadn't done my homework, that I hadn't researched things properly, that I didn't actually know it was Eddie Irvine in a Ferrari rather than Michael Schumacher in the other Ferrari that had been fleetingly shown on the screen, then I would be genuinely worried.

'There is a world of difference between you, sitting in the comfort of your cloistered home, in your living room in front of your 26-inch colour set, having excluded your loved ones from the room so that you can concentrate on what is happening – and at the start someone goes off. "Why didn't that prat say that Frentzen has gone onto the grass?" The answer is that I am looking at Coulthard, Häkkinen and Schumacher on this part of the screen, rather than that part of the screen, and talking about them because that's where the real action is. And I don't regard that as a mistake.

‘ And that piece of water on the right is the Olympic rowing strip, which I have walked down ’

'Any mistakes that I make are instantly heard as mistakes in Australia, Canada, New Zealand, all these other places, and I probably don't realise I've made a mistake, but if I did there's nothing I could do about it because there is no point in my saying "hang on a minute, it wasn't Häkkinen, it was Coulthard. I did realise all the time it was Coulthard because of his helmet" – and describe the difference between their helmets. By the time you've said all that you're now looking at Frentzen who has burst into flames and I'm saying nothing about it.'

Even taking all this as mitigation (which it is), many of the blunders are truly thunderous and that is why they decorate this book. To achieve a balance I should have included some of the word-perfect and highly authoritative commentary that in reality makes up most of Murray's output but, as someone remarked about something else altogether, readers can console themselves with the thought that, if I had, this book would have cost much more to buy and taken a lot longer to read.

'You've got the matting, the water coming through, blank
screens – and he's still talking.'

11

FRACTION OF THE ACTION

If you want to appreciate how good Murray Walker really is, you need to go back to what historians call original research with primary documents. In his case, these are the commentaries themselves as he did them, dealing with whatever came along and however fast it came along. This is by definition a personal selection, and I offer it in tribute to his speed of reaction, his ability to improvise and, ultimately, to how he betrayed his emotion but did not lose control of it.

Italian Grand Prix, Monza, 7 September 1969. The circuit was famous for slip-streaming and into the last lap four drivers – Jackie Stewart (Matra), Jochen Rindt (Lotus), Jean-Pierre Beltoise (Matra) and Bruce McLaren (McLaren) – were doing that. 'Four cars virtually together. Down to the Parabolica they come ... it's Rindt going through ... Beltoise going through ... it's going to

be a French Matra to win ... it's over the line ... AND IT'S ALMOST A DEAD HEAT! It's Jackie Stewart.'
It was and it finished Rindt 0.08 seconds behind, Beltoise 0.17 and McLaren 0.19.

French Grand Prix, Dijon, 1 July 1979. Gilles Villeneuve (Ferrari) and René Arnoux (Renault) contested second place over the final two laps. It was as if a sublime madness had seized both men. 'The French crowd is going mad ... and Villeneuve just [*goes inside, locks brakes*] ... INCREDIBLE. Into the last lap and Arnoux does it, does he? Villeneuve locks up and Arnoux's on the inside ... they bang wheels ... he's off, he's off, he's back again, René Arnoux off the circuit ... and Villeneuve is back, he's in second position.'

It finished Jabouille winning, Villeneuve at 14.59 seconds, Arnoux at 14.83.

Monaco Grand Prix, Monte Carlo, 23 May 1982. Alain Prost (Renault) led but crashed by the harbour on the second last lap. Riccardo Patrese (Brabham) led but spun. Didier Pironi (Ferrari) led but stopped on the last lap with an electrical fault. 'Is that Pironi in the tunnel? He's stationary! My Goodness! The third leader in two laps.' Andrea de Cesaris (Alfa Romeo) led and 'that is de Cesaris's car. De Cesaris would have taken the lead when Pironi – so that means that Derek Daly can win this race – Patrese could win!' It finished Patrese, Pironi classified second, de Cesaris classified third.

Australian Grand Prix, Adelaide, 26 October 1986.
Nigel Mansell (Williams) was moving comfortably towards the World Championship. He was running third on lap 64 (of 82) when, at 180mph … 'AND LOOK AT THAT [*a rear tyre explodes, thrashing like an octopus*]. Oh that is – that's Mansell. THAT IS NIGEL MANSELL. And the car absolutely shattered [*the car is bucking from side to side*]. He's fighting for control. You can see what's happened.' It finished Prost (McLaren), who took the championship, Nelson Piquet (Williams), Stefan Johansson (Ferrari).

Japanese Grand Prix, Suzuka, 21 October 1990. Ayrton Senna (McLaren) had pole position, was angry that it wouldn't be moved to the side of the track he wanted, and had Prost (Ferrari) alongside him. They had crashed bitterly at this race the year before. Green. 'And Senna sprints away but Alain Prost takes the lead. It's happened. Alain Prost has taken the advantage [*as they surge towards the first corner Senna jinks out from behind Prost*]. Senna is trying to go through on the inside [*they collide*] and it's happened immediately [*there's a dust storm being churned in the run off area at the first corner*]. This is AMAZING! Senna goes off at the first corner but what has happened to Prost? [*the Ferrari looms, motionless, as the dust storm settles*]. He's gone off too. Well, that is amazing but I fear absolutely – predictable.'

And it doesn't matter how that race finished.

Japanese Grand Prix, Suzuka, 13 October 1996. Damon Hill (Williams) was leading the race and only needed to stay where he was to win the World Championship [*shadows fall across the track as Hill nears completion of the final lap*]. 'This is going to be a mighty emotional occasion for a lot of people, not the least of whom is myself, and Damon Hill will be concentrating in the cockpit there [*in a curve*] but when he comes out of it his arms will go up, the helmet will come off [*camera cuts to pit lane wall where Georgie Hill is holding a black and white placard* DAMON WORLD CHAMPION 1996]. That's his wife Georgie. She's seeing her husband become World Champion. Now she's seeing him win the Japanese Grand Prix because he is almost home ... [*voice rising*] ... Damon Hill exits the chicane and wins the Japanese Grand Prix [*car darts across the track towards the pit wall and the team there*] and I've got to stop [*tiny pause*] because I've got a lump in my throat.'

Later, Murray interviewed Hill who said 'I was driving along and I could hear you in my head.'

We all can.

Hungarian Grand Prix, Hungaroring, 19 August 2001.
Michael Schumacher had been the engine room in
Ferrari's revival and now, in splendid isolation, he
prepared to win his second consecutive World
Championship for them. Schumacher is into the final
lap and Murray prefaces that by saying it was 'to re-
write Formula 1 history. Championship number four
coming up. Michael Schumacher:
final lap. Car: Ferrari ... and Michael
Schumacher comes out of Turn
Eleven into Turn Twelve. Thirteen is
coming up now ... it's a fourteen
corner lap. Michael Schumacher goes
into that last corner for the last time in the Hungarian
Grand Prix *[Schumacher is in the looping Turn Fourteen
which feeds him out onto the start-finish straight]*. He
exits the corner, he crosses the line. Michael
Schumacher wins! Michael Schumacher is World
Champion! *[Schumacher is brandishing his fist in
triumph.]* And Michael Schumacher, as ever, is
absolutely eu-ph-oric!'

*' I imagine the
conditions in those
cars are totally
unimaginable '*

And that was it, the last of Murray's championship
commentaries.

*'Murray and I were the only two people left in the circuit
and we were locked in . . .'*

12

SO YOUNG AT HEART

You'd see him stumping along and you knew by his movements that something was wrong. Ordinarily he walked with something approaching a military bearing, upright, firm, full of purpose. Now he stumped. You could see, too, if you looked closely that he was in pain and conceding nothing to that. In time he wore a tee-shirt with the legend *Yes I am Murray Walker and Yes I have had a hip operation* written across it, presumably because people were forever asking him about it. This may also have been a way of making light of it. He comes from a generation where misfortune is borne in silence.

Post surgery, in the early 1990s, there was a quick return to the military bearing. Keith Mackenzie remembers being with him in South Africa 'just after he'd had it done and he was amazing, almost back to normal. He gave himself some punishing physiotherapy to make sure he did get up and about as quickly as possible.'

I knew Murray was in pain because, with typical generosity, he had invited me down to his house to help me with a book I was writing on Mike Hailwood. During the lunch (when he had a single glass of claret and relished it) he said something *slightly* sharp about Hailwood and that was so out of character it had to be induced by the pain. I offer this as a measure of the man: that he said something even slightly sharp was so remarkable – as if, for a strange and fleeting moment he was no longer an English gentleman – that it struck me hard. (I've only met two or three other people like that in my life, one of whom was my grandfather.)

' *Tambay's hopes, which were previously nil, are now absolutely zero* '

That he was hyper active before and after the surgery is a cause of wonder. Listen to Roger Moody talking about the mid-1980s when Murray was in his 60s. At the end of each race abroad, the BBC had a 15-minute slot in which to send their own material from the track to London.

'We had to go and grab interviews with the good and the great. We would scramble down from our commentary boxes, which were of course on the opposite side of the track to the pits and the paddock. I had to grab

Murray almost by the collar and thrust him down the grandstand and through the tunnel under the track. All the punters – 100,000 of them – were coming the other way and Murray wasn't particularly young then. I used to force him through all these crowds. To be honest, I was in my thirties, he was a lot older and I really treated him like baggage. I'd

' A mediocre season for Nelson Piquet, as he is now known, and always has been '

push him in front of a camera and grab whoever the driver was. You'd think this is too much for him but the instant it was "London are recording, go" he was Mr Professional again. He asked the right questions in the right way and even if he did ask the wrong questions everyone loved him for it.

'An example of all this was Portugal, the final race in 1984. Niki Lauda and Alain Prost were both going for the World Championship and when Lauda won it we were very keen to get our interview. There had been nothing arranged for interviews. On behalf of the BBC I got a camera into a room at the start of the pit lane' – this was small, packed with people and imitating a proper interview room. 'We got Prost and Lauda sitting down there good as gold and we got our interview. You'd throw Murray into a situation like that and he'd cope with it. He'd do stand-ups and pieces to camera and there were very few retakes.'

Perhaps longevity is a hereditary thing and Mackenzie offers this intriguing insight. 'Murray's mum was, I think, 101 when she died. In her 90s she went into some sort of nursing home because she needed more than normal care and attention. Murray used to go to visit her regularly and often she'd say to him "Murray, you need to get your hair cut." She also said "Murray, I think I am going to get one of those new Ford Escorts. That should suit me quite well to do a little bit of running around in" and Murray would say "yes, mum, yes, I think that's a good idea."

'Possibly that's where he gets it from. Could well do. He's healthy. He goes to his local health club quite regularly and I think more so since he's had his hips

MURRAY'S MOMENTS
James Allen, ITV reporter

A couple of times Murray has come to me live when I wasn't expecting him. You remember Spa in 1998 and the huge pile-up just after the start? The delay before the re-start must have been an hour. By then we'd pretty much worked out who'd be taking that re-start and we were now facing a two-hour race, which is a long time. I went off to the loo and while I was in there Murray came over to me – there I was scrabbling around for my microphone ...

done. The thing that always amazes me is how energetic he is for his age.'

Murray himself explains that his mother was 'a very, very astute woman and she did very well on the Stock Exchange. She had a considerable amount of money of her own. I managed, when she was 96, to prise her out of her home and persuade her to go into a retirement place, a wonderful place which had the staff.'

Gerry Donaldson insists that 'the sport is Murray's fountain of youth. He's got the energy of a man half his age and he just loves it.'

Tony Jardine says 'the thing about Murray, for me, is that he has all his faculties. He's as bright as he was years ago and I've known him, what, 26, 27 years. There's been all this criticism about him making more and more mistakes – we know the down side of that, we know his detractors – but the fact is, that's part of the joy of Murray. It's not just his faculties, he's still got his sparkle. He still goes to the gym twice a week, he's still careful about his diet and he is still absolutely sharp. He has us all in stitches, he picks up on all the jokes, he makes jokes and tells stories himself.'

' There's only a second between them. One. That's how long a second is '

They had a quiet dinner together a couple of years ago. This was the conversation.

Jardine: 'I don't know when you're thinking of quitting, but you are the same as you were ten years ago. This is your life, this is what keeps you young.'

Walker: 'That's very nice of you but I want to quit before they start saying *get the old fool out*. I don't want to be pushed, I want to go graciously.'

That might be the perfect way to end this chapter, but my memories stray back to that first interview in 1982. He explained that he normally arrived at a Grand Prix on the Thursday and walked the track twice, once the way the cars went and once the other way – amazing what you might notice doing that. He drew his own map of the track and on that noted where the camera positions were (15 of them at Monza). He

' MURRAY'S MOMENTS
Roger Moody, former BBC producer

At Estoril one year, we'd done the commentary, we'd done our interviews and we'd gone back to the commentary box to take all Murray's notes down and clean up. We always left our box spick and span. The circuit was empty and we went to the gate. Murray and I were the only two people left in the circuit and we were locked in. We looked over towards the grandstands and the local fire brigade were there. We yelled at them to put up their turntable ladder and we scaled it to get out. '

recounted how before the previous Italian Grand Prix, as he'd been walking the track, he noticed a tiny flower growing in a crevice. He picked it, took it home and pressed it in a book just the way romantic teenagers do. If you are still doing this at the age of 58 you've discovered eternal youth or something very close to it.

James Allen put the matter reverently. 'He encourages young people and takes a delight in their success. He has stayed young at heart. You would not believe his age unless you saw his birth certificate. Inside him is a teenage boy going to see his first Grands Prix with Rosemeyer and Nuvolari in them – but he is also a very mature, wise man. He is a gentleman.'

Simon Taylor penetrated to the very soul of it. 'When you see something for the first time and you say *wow!* you have a genuine sense of wonder. A good journalist will go on saying *wow!* genuinely, and you will be able to communicate that. Now take the old cynical Fleet Street fellow in the bar trying to manufacture it – if he tries that, it doesn't work. In Murray's case, that sense of excitement – which communicates itself so well – is absolutely central to why he is entertaining.'

Walker only got the FULL *wow!* factor after he retired: on the grid just before the 2002 British Grand Prix. He felt the animal excitement there – when working he'd always been up in the commentary box.

The massive screen in Spain.

13

THE SOUNDS OF SILENCE

A television commentator will, given enough time, become more famous than a lot of the people he is talking about because they come and go and he remains, often for decades – cumulatively he's on the screen more than they are, anyway, even if it's just his voice. Murray Walker could not walk through the paddock at Silverstone without being semi-mobbed and I won't embarrass the drivers who could by naming them.

Colin Wilson, communications manager of the Motor Sport Association – the governing body in Britain – remembers exactly this. 'You'd never know Murray was a star to talk to him. Drivers are the obvious comparison. I know many drivers who I knew when they were little nippers and they don't give you the time of day now because they're too busy, too important, they have too many minders. I've never seen Murray with a minder!'

This is a crucial point. Murray was infinitely more famous than half the grid but he never flaunted that. To the contrary: he seemed to be constantly gazing at anonymous newcomers to the grid in something approaching awe. To Murray, every race was the exact rebirth of a passion and the most anonymous driver a guardian of that passion. *This* is what crossed your living room and talked directly to you. The fame came along with it too.

'A couple of years ago we just happened to be going the length of the Formula 1 paddock,' Colin Wilson says. 'He was probably going off to see somebody important like Bernie Ecclestone and I was going off to do something mundane like get the bins emptied in the photographers' zone. I decided to walk down with him because we were talking about rallying. It took us an hour and a quarter to get to the other end of the paddock!

'Formula 1 has almost become a victim of its own success. Every race you have traffic jams and nowhere to park and long walks and huge amounts of money. Murray has managed to stay very level-headed. If you ask him to tell a story he will almost always tell one against himself. He seems to relish recounting his own Colemanballs.' [This is a column of sporting gaffes in the magazine *Private Eye,* named after David Coleman.]

Do you think he has grown because the sport has grown or – in Britain and the Commonwealth countries – it has grown because of him?

'It's like a ladder. They climb up on top of each other. If he had not helped make motor racing popular then he wouldn't be as well-known as he is but the opposite's also true and it was true of James Hunt. He was more popular as Murray's fellow commentator than he ever had been as a driver, even in his championship year. He was far more widely known and respected for his views as a commentator. Murray's contribution is absolutely incalculable. He has probably done more than any other single person to popularise motor racing – and rallying, too, because in his early days he did a lot of rally commentating as well.'

'That was exactly the same place where Senna overtook Nannini that he didn't overtake Alain Prost'

Gerry Donaldson mints a lovely phrase for how Murray has popularised Grand Prix racing: 'leadership through enthusiasm – he's kind of a cheerleader.'

Britain has nurtured various commentators who became synonymous with their sports including Eddie Waring and Rugby League, Peter O'Sullevan and horse racing, Peter Alliss and golf, John Arlott and cricket, and Dan Maskell and Wimbledon. Murray Walker, as someone said, made you tune in to motor racing. Whether by accident or design, these people and their voices mirrored the very essence of their sport: Waring blunt and northern, O'Sullevan's voice rippling with speed, Alliss pondering golf's byways, Arlott chewing his way across the landscape of olde England.

Motorsport is by definition a sort of detonation and Murray detonated every two weeks. He could make a routine pit stop by the leader of a race sound like the most astonishing thing the world had ever seen; he could turn a procession of cars circling the Hungaroring for an hour into a breathless sprint, and both were done so consummately that afterwards you wondered *how*. The naked excitement of any race – the concentration of power, speed, ambition, uncertainty – flowed up from the track to him and through him to you. He didn't portray a race, he stood there in the commentary box acting as a transmitter.

'If I had to describe Murray in one sentence,' Barrie Gill will say, 'it's that he's one of the world's greatest enthusiasts and most diligent researchers but a genuine personality. There are people in television today who think they are personalities but Murray *is* one. A dinner with him, a drink with him, sitting next to him on a plane is always a pleasure. Murray is a brand: a brand of excitement, enthusiasm, the occasional mistake – but I defy anybody in the world, including Martin Brundle, not to make a mistake in two hours. Murray has not set a standard for how to do it, he has set a style.'

He also has an ego. This was glimpsed when he told me he wrote a book with Mike Hailwood – Murray doing all the work – and Hailwood wasn't particularly bothered even to read the manuscript. Murray found that difficult to comprehend because, if the situation had been reversed, his ego would have compelled him to read it in case the manuscript didn't reflect well on him. I think he enjoyed being well-known, and certainly enjoyed the benefits of that in the motor racing world, but he didn't wallow in it any more than he did the flaunting.

It is easy to forget how much the world has changed, easy to forget that Murray's formative years were the 1930s when many public aspects of British life were gentler, more restrained, more polite, more respectful, less destructive. The notion of a two-bit television or radio 'interviewer' shouting down Ministers of the Crown on a current affairs programme would have been regarded as both incomprehensible *and* disgusting. In absolute contrast, Murray has shown basic respect to everyone he's ever interviewed.

'I took him to dinner recently,' Linda Pattisson says, 'because he was doing a photo shoot to promote a video game. He was staying in town and I said "let's go for dinner." I had invited him but no way would he allow me to pay. It was an Italian restaurant. Murray ordered his food, the waiter stepped back and said "ooooh, you're Murray Walker." He didn't know the face but he knew the voice. Then he said "well, are you Murray Walker?" and Murray said "I think so." Now every time I walk into that restaurant I get the most fantastic table.

'There was a sadness when I asked him if he was going to Goodwood this year [2001] and he said "I just can't because I feel I'm going to be rude to everybody." Stirling Moss can cover a room, go through it really quickly and it doesn't seem rude. Murray gets surrounded and you always feel you can approach him.' And people did, in ever increasing numbers, and almost immediately you'd hear that crackling, chuckling laughter and see that hand pumping out hand-shakes.

'He enjoys people. He is a people watcher. He's quite happy to sit in a café with you and watch other people. He's basically a journalist at heart: he enjoys finding out. Some people enjoy the fame, and they end up surrounding themselves with go-fers. I can think of one or two drivers who have done that. A lot of the way he behaves, his courtesy and his manners, rubs off on people around him. He is courteous to everybody, like going to dinner. In fact, the only petulance I've ever heard is when he's been cross about the shots being shown during a Grand Prix when a local editor is just showing, say, the leader and there's a fantastic battle going on behind.'

Sir Stirling Moss admits he is 'such a fan. I had to go to Rockingham [the new racing circuit in Northamptonshire] and he was speaking. He pointed out that Clive James said he commentated "as if my trousers are on fire" – but in truth he will be missed for this. Somebody asked him if he thought motor racing was boring now and Murray said "no way, there's *this* and *this* and *this.*" When I think about it, Murray can take a seriously tedious race and give it some interest. He is really a magician.'

Murray's courtesy was appreciated by Louise Goodman. 'How can you not get on with Murray? He's just such a sweet man. When I first started working in Formula 1, about my second race he came up and introduced himself. I was an absolute nobody and *he* introduced himself! When I went to work for Jordan he sent me a little hand-written note. *Congratulations on your new job and I hope it all goes well.* It was sincere and I've still got it. He's just the sweetest man, he really is. He is incredibly generous with his time and his knowledge. You can go to him and ask him anything.'

'*Either the car is stationary or it's on the move*'

Linda Pattisson says, however, that Murray 'has a value in himself and he understands value within the market place. He will never sell himself short. He'll say to me "I think that the contract I did with this particular company is not the right one. Can you look at it for me?" He is very direct about what's right and wrong.'

This matter of petulance, or mostly a complete lack of it, is taken up by Keith Mackenzie. 'Murray is a great chap, he's terrific to travel with, he's terrific company, he tells some wonderful stories, he's very entertaining and he's a caring person. I've never ever seen him lose his temper. He is always concerned about how everybody is working around him. He doesn't expect to be treated as a star. He's just one of the boys, one of the crew. He's very appreciative of anything anybody does for him and we all look after him, of course, but he doesn't expect anything.'

Eddie Stephens, who knew him in advertising, reinforces that. 'As a chap he was one of the very best and you could rely 100% on him every time – he was the best kind of business person too.'

Raymond Baxter agrees. 'He is an extremely nice man. He's very emotional. We had quite a lot of fun, one way or another. When they did him on *This Is Your Life* I appeared, and when they did me on *This Is Your Life* he appeared – and we each said nice things about each other.' So they got to say them twice, which is somehow apt because Murray has always said nice things about Baxter, and Baxter knows and appreciates that.

Before you gain the impression that Murray Walker is some kind of divinity, let me return to the Thunderous Blunders and recount a story of joint fallibility. One year at Hockenheim we decided to have dinner – a group of journalists and the BBC team – in a restaurant called, I think, the *Goldene Krone*, because we all knew it. The journalists were there (more or less) on time but after 30 or 40 minutes no sign of Murray and the BBC troupe. I went back to our hotel, which was nearby, and phoned his hotel, which was not nearby. He had left a message on the reception: *'if anybody rings, we are in the Goldene Krone'*. If I tell you that in and around Hockenheim there is more than one *Goldene Krone* you'll get the idea ...

The enthusiasm reached to the drivers. Johnny Herbert says 'Murray has always been the ultimate enthusiast and that's been the nice thing about him. You hear that when he's commentating. He's excited and it comes across that way. Yes, there are the mistakes which unfortunately is his trademark – but it's something that's been good for him as well. When he comes round to speak to you he is invariably polite and that's nice and that's rare. He has a very kind nature.'

This kindness extended to a certain leniency in the matter of criticism (although at the end of one Brazilian Grand Prix, a spectator ran on with the cars still going round and Murray shouted 'and there's a raving, raving lunatic'). 'Murray,' Roger Moody says, 'would never ever really criticise anybody. He comes from the old school and that's why everyone loves him.'

The old school commentators commented rather than sit in judgement and certainly did not cast themselves as judge, jury and executioner over the people in their remit. Nigel Roebuck, one of the senior British motorsport journalists, judged that 'Murray's genius is making a dull afternoon sound exciting. The thing I have never really understood about Murray is that there have been times when we have had people in the Press Room going to sleep – literally going to sleep – and then the race ends and Murray will come in, his eyes alight. People will say "wasn't it terrible?" and he'll say "what do you mean, it was fantastic." I can only presume he means it.'

There were exceptions, however. At Monaco in 2001, as Roebuck says, 'Murray came and put his arm round me and said "I don't suppose you enjoyed that much"' – Michael Schumacher won easily – 'and I said "no, I did not." He said "I can't say I did either, and I'm sad because it's my last Monaco."'

'You get the impression from listening to Murray that he likes everybody in the race – every team owner, every driver – and he approves of them and all the rest of it. Privately he does not and you know damn well there are people he absolutely does not like but that never comes through. There are times when I wish Murray would be a little more controversial. Conversely he could say he always had James with him to do that, and now Martin.'

On a personal note, I have never experienced anything but the kindness and courtesy so many people have already spoken about. You have to remember that he has seen everyone from Bernd Rosemeyer in 1937 all the way to here and as a consequence is himself living history. He was particularly helpful in a couple of bike racing books I did because he is living history in that too, and often enough was *there*. He takes a delight in sharing his knowledge and takes such things very seriously. That crackling, chuckling laughter can fill his book-lined study hour after hour, and does.

Inevitably, the British Grand Prix at Silverstone in 2001 became a place of personal farewell. As the cars waited on the grid he moved into his customary crescendo.

'Now is Michael Schumacher going to cut across the front of Mika Häkkinen? He's famous for that. Three lights. Four lights. Five laps! Pause. GO! GO! GO!' Instanteously, as he said 'laps' he knew he'd blundered but verbally drove through, just as he'd always done. It was a precious moment, charged with all manner of nostalgia.

The nostalgia was everywhere. When the cars were finally silent a crowd of hundreds gathered outside the warren of buildings and vans where the television companies work and he came out onto a platform to speak to them. He was cheered. 'Thank you all very much,' he said quietly, in a voice which was somehow humble and touched. He held a small bottle of mineral water and fiddled with it almost as if, amazingly, he might have been nervous of speaking in public. 'I have had 52 wonderful years, the best of them have been at the British Grand Prix – at Silverstone and at Aintree and at Brands Hatch.' There was a quaver in his voice of, I suspect, sudden sadness he was finding it hard to conceal. 'You can only do so much as an individual but if you've got the love and respect of the people you are talking to it makes it a very easy job. I've loved every second of it. Thank you very much.' They cheered again and clapped their hands above their heads, and he turned away and was gone down the metal stairwell, still holding the bottle of mineral water.

' Alain Prost is in a commanding second place '

He wouldn't make his final farewell as a commentator for five more Grands Prix – at the United States at Indianapolis. That was especially poignant because it was on 30 September, just nineteen days after the terrorist attack on New York and Washington. The poignancy was two-fold. This was the first international sporting event in America since the attack, with all that involved, and it was a demonstration that the civilised world had not been stopped from going about its lawful – and pleasurable – business. Murray Walker's end was also a renewal – a beginning of the rest of the Formula 1 story. It could scarcely have been more apt. He had been a Grands Prix commentator since 1949, the year before the modern World Championship even began.

He might have chosen the last race of 2001 – the Japanese Grand Prix on 14 October – to do the deed, but preferred Indianapolis instead. Forgive him. The time gap meant that the United States GP was broadcast in the United Kingdom in the evening, maximising the number of viewers who'd be saying their own farewells. For British fans Japan happens in the middle of the night, Japan is a long flight away and Suzuka – a track of rudimentary facilities – is lost in the equivalent of the Midlands.

Starbucks has it over sushi every day.

And that's where Murray went. When he got there, it did not prevent some grandstand spectators draping a white banner over the railing in front of them which beseeched:

MURRAY
DON'T GO GO GO!

But he would.

ITV anchor man Jim Rosenthal (left) with Martin Brundle and 'Mr Motor Racing'.

14

NORMAL SERVICE RESUMED

Before we reach Indianapolis it's time to listen to Jim Rosenthal who, since ITV took over coverage of Grand Prix racing, has been the programme's anchor man. Rosenthal is a perceptive man, but, even more than that, he came to it as an outsider.

'I got into Grand Prix racing purely because ITV took it over. I think it's fairly common knowledge that it was all lined up for Steve Rider to do it, but for whatever reason – and I'm very, very grateful! – he decided not to leave the dear old BBC. I had a passing knowledge of the subject. I was told I'd got the job in the January and of course the season started in the March. When I got the job I thought: *well, I'm going to give it a good old go and no matter how few I do I'm going to enjoy every one. There is no point in pretending I know everything about Grand Prix racing* – because obviously I didn't.'

The commentators we've already met – Tony Jardine

and Simon Taylor and James Allen – were long steeped in the culture. If someone said *quallies* or *keep it on the island or The Rat* they wouldn't need anyone to translate. Rosenthal, coming straight in from the cold, might appear utterly lost when anyone on the programme started talking like that, as they surely would. OK, he wasn't going to commentate but he was going to be fielding all sorts of other situations, some possibly approaching him at high speed and from oblique angles.

Rosenthal, a highly experienced professional, decided to make a virtue of his situation. 'It can be a strength, lacking expert knowledge because you approach it as a journalist rather than getting involved in, say, the tyre compounds.' The journalist sees, by training and thought process, what is important and what is not. 'I think,' he adds, 'I was fortunate in some ways in that I also had a new audience who were quite happy to learn the sport with me. With hindsight, I am sure that was an advantage.

'I had met Murray a couple of times but as an acquaintance, nothing more. I can remember ringing him up and saying "I'm sorry old chap, you've got me" and he said "I'm absolutely delighted. Anything you want" – in typical Murray terms – "just ask." As it turned out, I did ask many times subsequently.

'I do vividly remember that first Grand Prix, which was the Australian at Melbourne. It's the only event I've ever done before or since where I've not slept the night before because it was so daunting. I can remember walking across Albert Park [to the track] thinking *what have I let myself in for here?* I am sure there were quite a few people thinking *well, he's going to crash and burn doing this one ON THE FIRST BEND* ...

'We did it, we got through it and at the end of the weekend we were in the TV compound [the cordoned-off area used by TV crews and personnel at a race]. Murray put his arm round me and said "you didn't put a foot wrong." I'd probably put a couple of feet wrong, you know, here and there but it was such a reassuring thing to come from him. In fact I'll use the word fantastic.'

Rosenthal got through it and by the time the highlights programme was put together he was confident enough to set the tone for the years to come, although – judged by his relaxed subsequent mastery of it – he seemed a little stiff at this initial moment, as if he was carefully working his way in. Mind you, he said almost softly 'hello, and welcome to the highlights of the Australian Grand Prix' as if he'd been doing nothing else for years. He explained that apart from the action on the track 'we'll be very busy behind the scenes as well' and then introduced Jardine and Taylor as the new resident experts. After some preliminary items of background he said 'let's join your commentators Martin Brundle and [voice rising] Murray Walker.'

To which Murray said, as the picture cut to the grid: 'So, the heat haze arising from the 700 horsepower engines ... 21 cars down there ... when the lights go out it is go ...'

Yes, *Murray* had been doing nothing else for years but never mind. Normal service had been resumed.

Soon enough, he and Rosenthal would be functioning as pivotal parts of the team and interacting so smoothly that it all seemed as if it was meant to be.

'The one thing that gets to me occasionally is when people just talk about Murray's mistakes and Murray's gaffes,' Rosenthal says. 'I mean, he is a very, very classy journalist and also a very, very classy television performer. He's a brilliant wordsmith, his voice is excellent, nice sense of drama, he always knew when to raise the voice and when to lower it: these are things that you can't really teach and Murray had them in abundance. A lot of his considerable professional qualities tend to get glossed over with people only talking about the mistakes.

'He is the only person I know who has profited from making mistakes (chuckle). In our business, after every little mistake you make, people say "what the bloody hell did you say that for?" – and we all make mistakes, of course we do. In fact, when you do make a mistake you say to *yourself*, "God, what did I say that for?" Murray has actually swung it round and used it as a plus.

'It was absolutely reassuring to have him there and it was reassuring in many ways. I can remember saying to my bosses before he came – and before I even knew I was going to get the job of presenting it – "listen, you've got to get Murray Walker across." That was all everybody was saying to me: "You must have Murray." So not only was he a reassurance [in terms of experience and ability to cope with anything, as we have seen] but he eased the passage of Formula 1 from the BBC to ITV. He was the biggest single factor, I think, in that he was a constant.

'If ITV hadn't got him, I would go so far as to say that it wouldn't have been the success it has been. He brought his fan club and he brought people with him [the BBC audience who'd lived it through him all these years]. Even now, never mind then, you'll hear someone saying "oh the bloody advertisements", so to have him was a comforting factor, both to the viewers and to those who worked with him. Mr Motor Racing was there.'

Keith Mackenzie has already said how easily Murray adapted to the complexity of the advert breaks but Rosenthal sees it in a subtly different way.

'I have grown up with adverts but it wasn't easy for him. To most people who come across from the BBC, the advertisements are like smoke bombs in some respects, but he got better and better with it, to the point where at the end it came across as something quite natural. And getting in and out of the adverts is a skill, especially covering motor racing. To be honest, any live sport that you leave, you leave at your peril. The best second-guesser in the world isn't going to get it right every time.

'Again, there is a misconception that you miss things. All right, in real time you do but thirty seconds later you see it and if it's done skilfully you almost don't see the join. I've heard that in Germany they go "ah, we are twenty minutes into the race, now it's time for our six minutes of adverts" no matter what's happening on the track. "Press that button, thank you very much, we'll see you in six minutes." At least we have bent over backwards to try and ensure that we don't miss anything.'

That was partly Murray, who early on discovered the knack of getting in and out of those things by weaving them into the fabric of the commentary. *Don't go away, we'll be back in a minute* in a voice promising many delights to come.

Rosenthal has never had a cross word with Murray – 'and his stamina is astonishing. I have seen him doing the early mornings and late nights in Formula 1, which people don't know about, and he's always been sharp and he's always been perky.'

This is not as serious as it sounds but needs a word of explanation. You do sometimes have late-ish nights, socialising or perhaps at some sponsorship event. You do often have the dawn drive to the track in the hire car to get in before the traffic seizes in all directions.

'I was at a couple of dinners with him – he seemed to have a few farewell dinners and farewell functions – and I have always been struck by the affection that people have for him across the board. Nobody comes up to you and says "what a horrible bastard he is." In motor racing – and also in television – you will almost inevitably get someone who *will* come up and tell you someone is an X!, a Y! or a Z! The two businesses are obviously very highly competitive and they promote the odd snake in the grass – let's put it that way – but they don't bite Murray. I think one reason is that he doesn't say many unkind things about people, either.'

The point has already been covered, that Murray hesitates to criticise and, in that, he is true to his formative years. Who remembers Waring or O'Sullevan or Alliss or Arlott or Maskell wielding the hatchet? You don't remember because they didn't or, if they did, it was done rarely and discreetly. Jim Rosenthal accepts the premise but expands it into an unexpected area which has particular relevance to Murray.

'Thinking about those people you mentioned – Waring and so on – I firmly believe that individuals on television, either as commentators or presenters, will not dominate sports any more, full stop. Sport has become so fragmented and that means you won't get a Voice of Motor Racing or a Voice of Football or a Voice of Cricket. You'll get a lot of good performers but not those giants like Murray and Arlott and O'Sullevan – and Richie Benaud, who is still a giant in cricket. I am sure that Murray was one of the last.'

M. Walker Esq, gentleman.

15

'THAT'S IT, FOLKS'

ITV's coverage of the final race began with Murray and Michael Schumacher reciting '... now the boot is on the other Schumacher'. I want to recreate the circumstances of this because they are extremely revealing.

Lynden Swainston, a motor racing insider for many years – she used to handle a great deal of Formula 1's travel, for instance – felt that when the BBC lost the contract to ITV to broadcast the Formula 1 races, Murray's contribution should be recognised. She had approached Bernie Ecclestone who agreed. There was a party and Ecclestone presented Murray with a trophy for services to motorsport.

Now, moving towards Indianapolis, she spoke to Ecclestone again. 'I asked if we could organise a farewell for Murray. Bernie said "yes, no problem at all" and asked where we should have it. I said I'd like to do it in the Paddock Club [the exclusive hospitality unit] and he agreed to check it out with Paddy McNally [who runs the Club through the Allsport Management company]. He did that. I then faxed the Paddock Club and they came back saying could I list what we wanted and, because it was Murray, they would be happy to provide it. Allsport laid on drinks and snacks.

'Murray didn't know about it but he said he had a feeling something was going on. He'd brought his wife Elizabeth to that race and I told her on the Thursday morning – I had breakfast with her – that something was happening. I said "it is obviously essential that you're there and part of it." She agreed – she's in the background most of the time.

'It was on the Saturday at 6.0. Jim Rosenthal went to get Elizabeth that afternoon because she hadn't been to the track. She was given pride of place at the front, which made Murray very weepy, I think, when he saw her. There was a huge array of people. We had decided to limit it to the British teams and press [some hopes!] and so we had 300 small Union Jacks printed. Everyone who was invited had a sticky Union Jack on their FOCA pass. That's how the Paddock Club let them in. All the Brits turned up and a most amazing amount of people I hadn't expected – Jean Todt and Ross Brawn from Ferrari, for example. I invited all the drivers and I didn't expect many to turn up. Michael came, which was a great surprise to me, every British driver, the

Jordan drivers turned up, Flavio [Briatore] came, Bernie came. In fact, Bernie was the first person to arrive, with Flavio, and they sat right at the front and he stayed throughout the whole thing. It was a most amazing occasion. ITV had put together a series of clips of Murray's greatest moments, which they showed and which had everybody in tears at the end. Tony Jardine hosted it and he got quite a few of the drivers to read out Murray's worst moments.'

Ann Bradshaw, like Lynden Swainston an insider these many years – as a popular, efficient and sympathetic Press Officer – was there because she'd been asked to look after the spare microphone. 'Murray was standing, TJ [Tony Jardine] was doing his bit as compere and every so often a guest would come up and say something – but the organisers didn't want Murray or TJ to have to hold another microphone, for the guests. That's what I was doing. Like a good girl, I popped forward, gave the guest a microphone and, when they'd finished, took it back off them. Everybody was there ...'

Jardine was doing, in his own words, 'the spiel – it had to be a person who knew Murray well, who could keep the thing running and, hopefully, make it funny. It wasn't meant to be solemn or anything – although we had to tread carefully in one sense, because it was post September 11. There was a fantastic turnout. You've got Bernie Ecclestone sitting right underneath your podium looking straight up into you, and the team bosses and so on. Everyone was in there, which shows the affection Murray was held in by everyone. We were all surprised by the extent of that – almost shocked, to be honest.

'All the top people in Formula 1 are in this one room and I thought to hell with it, we've got to go for this. While we looked at his achievements we had to make it light-hearted. We had bits of video out-takes, Murray sitting down, and I did go for it. My opening gambit was "welcome to the final meeting of the Murray Walker Appreciation Society." That got a chuckle but clearly Mr. George [Tony George, circuit owner] felt there were regular meetings of this 'Society'! When he stood up at the end to give Murray a brick from the original brickyard circuit – Murray was overawed by that, incidentally – George went into full, serious mode. He said "I'd like to address the members of the Murray Walker Appreciation Society ..."

'Anyway, you had a lot of Brits in there, team owners and drivers and so on, who were chuckling away during this 'presentation' and enjoying it. I'm taking Murray to task – well, taking the mickey – and his wife's sitting down there. You know how Murray puts his hands on his hips? He did that and he said "come on Jardine, I'm ready for anything." I said "in the early days your wife used to be allowed to come to the races, carry your clipboard and all the rest of it.

Latterly you haven't wanted her around." He made some remark and she laughed back and on it went.

'My idea was to get the drivers to come up. Coulthard did and Irvine did. I gave them a little cue card which had a Murray quote on it and they had to say that. They did really well.'

And then, of course, there was Schumacher. As Ms Bradshaw says, 'Schumacher knew Murray – everybody knows Murray! They'd got a lot of people to recite Murrayisms.' Yes, and here was Schumacher's recital.

Imagine this: an elegant marquee, Jardine standing behind a lectern grinning, and Murray, in shirt sleeves, leaning an elbow onto the lectern. Schumacher, in jeans and a red Ferrari top, holds the microphone which Ms Bradshaw has just given him. Schumacher holds Jardine's cue card and leans towards Murray, who puts a paternal arm around his shoulders. They read it together – in unison and close harmony, actually – culminating in "... and now the boot's on the other Schumacher." It got thunderous applause, Schumacher handed the card back to Jardine and he and Murray shook hands. You could feel the affection in Schumacher's smile.

'I didn't think Michael would actually come up,' Jardine says, 'but he did because he had a lot of time for Murray.'

'The most amazing thing,' Lynden Swainston says, 'was that the girls who work for Paddy McNally asked if they could come and they stood at the back. At the end one of them, a girl called Isabel Kaufmann, came up to me and she said "I'd never understood the bond with the British people in the paddock. I've never seen anything like this before and it has left me very, very moved."'

Ah yes, and the pay-off. The next day Murray had to interview Michael Schumacher, and Jardine reconstructs their conversation.

Schumacher: 'Murray, I'm not sure about something. Did you enjoy yesterday?'

Murray: 'Yeah, yeah, great, thanks for coming.'

Schumacher: 'No, no, I mean Tony Jardine. I thought he was cruel. Why was he talking like that about you all the time – especially when your wife was there?'

Murray: 'No, no, that's our British humour. They were laughing with me, not at me.'

Schumacher: 'Oh! I'll never ever understand British humour.'

The funny peculiar part, Jardine thought, was that during the presentation 'every time I'd looked over, Schumacher had been laughing but he probably had not connected with it at all.' Nor perhaps that Schumacher means shoe maker [strictly, it should be Schuhmacher but never mind] and that makes the boot ever more inappropriate.

In a way, the ceremony at Indianapolis was a distillation of everything Murray represented.

Listen to Ann Bradshaw. 'About ten years ago I took my mother for a special birthday treat – her eightieth – to a very nice hotel-spa-leisure club in the New Forest which Nigel Mansell has used a lot. We were there for a long weekend and on the Saturday afternoon the phone rang. I thought, apart from my family, who knows I'm here? I picked it up and this voice – that you cannot mistake – said: "Ann Bradshaw, what are you doing at my health centre?!"

'Murray's personal stuff has always been looked after by my mate Linda Pattisson at CSS. Linda happened to have rung Murray and he had just got in. "Oh," she said, "you sound a bit out of breath." He said "I've just been for a swim. I've got a wonderful new health centre up the road at Chewton Glen. Elizabeth and myself have joined." Linda said: "I can't believe it. That's where Ann Bradshaw has taken her mum for a birthday treat." Murray said "right, I'll take them out to lunch." He rang and, that Sunday, Murray and Elizabeth came along and treated my mother, who is an enormous Murray fan, to lunch. The lunch was lovely and we had a swim together. Since then we have gone down specially to take them out to lunch.

'He's one of those people you can't help but love. I've always known him well because I've had the pleasure of dealing with his favourite drivers – people like Nigel, Damon and DC, who he's become very close to. He has always been such a gentleman and they adored him. I've never had a driver, team owner or whoever refuse when I've said "Murray Walker wants to interview you." The foreign drivers and journalists all know him as well. We were shocked when we arrived in Adelaide for the first time [in 1985] to find them even bigger Murray fans than the UK. We didn't know where Adelaide was! We didn't think the Australians were really interested, we didn't even know that their TV took Murray and James.'

Reflecting, Roger Moody – who worked with him for so long and saw him in good times and bad – expresses these sentiments precisely. 'Murray is one of life's consummate gentlemen. Not only will there never be another Murray Walker – and there shouldn't be – but those who follow have an absolutely unenviable task.

'When I was chairman of the school parent teachers' association – the secondary school that my lad went to – I used to organise fund-raising evenings and we decided to have one on Grand Prix racing. I got a film from the BBC and Ron Dennis came along with a mock-up McLaren and Murray came along. Murray would not take a penny for doing that. And that is the measure of the man. He was prepared to give of his time and his expertise and his knowledge. How can you not be charmed? A lot of commentators and presenters and television quote personalities unquote could learn a lot from Murray.

'In terms of the Grand Prix scene I don't think that Murray sees nationalities. He sees good, excellent and sometimes indifferent drivers but it doesn't even enter his head that there might be an Argentinian driver whose country may have caused problems during the Falklands war or a Japanese driver whose country might have caused problems in the Second World War, or an Austrian driver. That has no relevance at all and why should it? In fact I don't remember him having a bad word to say about anybody. He was always courteous.

'The greatest accolade that anyone can pay any commentator of Murray's stature and status is this: I don't recall anyone, absolutely anyone – from the lowest mechanic to Bernie Ecclestone, and on the way through I'm talking about drivers and team managers and sponsors – saying anything really bad about Murray, well, bad at all.' This accolade was physically expressed on the Saturday at Indianapolis.

Moody's conclusion: Murray is 'one of life's truly great and unrepeatable characters.'

Simon Taylor, himself a broadcaster and co-author of a book with Murray, catches the essentials beautifully. One year Taylor was doing a scene-setter from Silverstone for Radio 4 'and somebody in the studio was saying something like "there isn't a British motor racing driver now who is held in real affection". I said "yes, but there is somebody in motorsport. As far as I am concerned there are three great British figures the public have taken to their hearts – the Queen Mother, Elton John and Murray Walker."'

There remained Indianapolis and the 2001 United States Grand Prix.

Jim Rosenthal moved straight into the fact that it was Murray's last race and trailed a 'very special Murray Meets at 7.0 your time.' It was part of a series he'd been doing over the years, and this one had been pre-filmed in the study of his Hampshire home, with its memorabilia and shelves full of motor racing books. He guards his collection zealously and, years ago when I was writing a motor cycling book and wanted to borrow a rare autobiography of a rider called Jim Redman, Murray said "sorry, I can't lend it to you. I've lost so many books over the years like that. But tell you what – there's a photocopying shop in the village. Why not do that?" It took less than 30 minutes to complete the copying of the whole book and at 2p a sheet didn't break the bank either. The point: he was torn between his natural courtesy of helping someone, and protecting his collection, and found the perfect compromise.

The study is a quiet room, and also a workplace. He guards the collection for reasons beyond nostalgia. He needs all manner of reference material because, as we have seen, he is extraordinarily careful about doing his homework. (In the study are bound volumes of the motor bike magazine his dad edited and a mutual friend once said he'd take them off Murray's hands because old stuff like that wasn't worth much anymore. 'I bet!' Murray said. He is nobody's fool. The volumes are still there.)

Now he sat in an armchair, a dark blue ITV F1 shirt on, and explained that this final guest was not only his best friend but constant companion for the 52 years he'd been commentating. Straight-faced, he said 'he's a super bloke, got a great sense of humour.' He continued in that vein for a while. It was so exquisitely crafted that you had to be thinking: who on earth can it be?

It was of course himself and the camera panned to another armchair where sat Murray Walker but wearing a bright blue shirt.

He interviewed himself and – wonderfully – the dark-shirted Murray wondered if he and his father George had ever raced against each other.

'Actually, my father's name was Graham,' said the bright-shirted one with a masterly grin. Only big men can take the mickey out of themselves (are you listening, Michael?) and only very big men can genuinely enjoy doing it.

The bright-shirted one, suddenly becalmed by nostalgia, finished 'thank you for being with me all these years.'

There remained the race itself. He previewed it with an outpouring of enthusiasm – 'fantastic' stadium, 'mammoth' crowd and so on – and then counted the red lights ... three ... four ... five' and – you know what he said next. You can hear it. After that he slipped effortlessly into the commentary but somehow, in a way which is difficult to define, he was carrying just enough enthusiasm to suggest it was his first race. Not too much, just enough. This cannot, absolutely cannot, have been a man in his late seventies.

Häkkinen won from Schumacher.

Brundle said he was speaking for tens of millions of people round the world when 'I say thank-you to Murray for what you have done for Formula 1.'

Murray said that after 52 years of Grand Prix racing he wanted to go out on a high note, to be 'euphoric about the fact that we had just seen a great race.' Brundle, moved, patted him on the back. Murray, eyes almost hooded, said 'well, that's it folks. That's the last from me. All I can say is it always has been a pleasure and I hope you will enjoy Grand Prix racing from now on.' He was very close to tears.

Of the millions and millions of words he'd hammered out of himself down the decades, he chose the simplest and most appropriate of them all to be the very last.

'Goodbye.'

ENDPIECE: MURRAY AND ME

Some people grow up within motor racing and some people come to it (forgive me) by accident. Murray Walker was my accident. My father had been an avid Grand Prix follower – and he'd been to Le Mans for the 24-hour race a time or two – but I was too submerged in cricket to notice much else. I batted a bit, and I bowled leg breaks and googlies which many a batsman delighted in hitting many a mile. I played rugby like the coward that I am. I ran, but not always with or towards the ball.

I was born in Newcastle and educated in Norfolk at a boarding school where the headmaster felt that boys should be playing sport, climbing trees and being in hot pursuit of the Austrian au pair girls who came to learn English. The rigours of academic study were, let us say, subsidiary to those other imperatives. It was this same headmaster who, two weeks before the crucial O level examinations, informed us that he had been teaching us the wrong syllabus in Religious Knowledge for the whole year but we must not worry that we wouldn't be able to answer any of the questions. He had looked up the examination rules and, since we were all already entered, we would have to turn up, sit for twenty minutes and then we could leave en masse. We did.

In those distant, dream-like days you could get a job without a daunting array of O and A levels, which explains how I started my working life as a general news reporter in Newcastle in 1962. Some twenty years later, via the *Sunday Express* in Manchester, I'd reached the sportsdesk of the *Daily Express* in London.

Curiously, for years motorsport had been considered news and Grand Prix reports appeared on news pages. By now it had reached us at the back of the paper. The *Express* of course had a motor racing correspondent (who also wrote about production cars, a legacy of when this was news) and a bike racing correspondent as well.

In 1976, as it happened, the Swedish Grand Prix and the Isle of Man TT virtually overlapped and so did Le Mans. With the two correspondents otherwise engaged, the situation was vacant. Knowing nothing whatsoever about it except that a lot of spectators had been killed there years before, I volunteered to go.

Knowing nothing, as travel writer Bill Bryson has observed, is a 'strangely wonderful position to be in'.

What I discovered was that motorsport can be dangerous: a restaurant owner from Strasbourg, a private entrant, was killed, and I've never forgotten this, or that it can happen. I also discovered that motor racing is fascinating, there are worse places to be than mid-France in mid-summer, and year after year I went back for more, notebook in hand.

As described earlier in the book, I became curious about this Murray Walker and his commentaries which, even then, were generating comment – so I went to interview him. Afterwards, he dutifully posed on a motorbike in his drive while an *Express* photographer took pictures. I wrote the piece, it appeared and I thought no more about it.

In June 1982 the USA Detroit and Canadian Grands Prix were back-to-back and the correspondents couldn't go: another situation vacant. Well, yes, I volunteered again and I've been writing about it ever since. At the start in Canada, incidentally, the young Italian Riccardo Paletti was killed, which itself might have been enough to turn me away from motorsport forever but, sub-consciously, perhaps I had been prepared by that restaurant owner from Strasbourg. I stayed.

Neither Murray nor James Hunt were on the trip to North America because the timing of the races fell in Britain's evening, the coverage wasn't live and they could cope easily enough from the studio in London. As a consequence I didn't see Murray again until the Dutch Grand Prix immediately afterwards.

The early part of the season had been wracked – and nearly wrecked – by a power struggle between FISA (as it was then) and FOCA, the Constructors' Association. For a newcomer and an outsider like me, this was fiendishly complicated, horribly political and a potential minefield. I dreaded writing about it and confided this to Murray, who said: 'If that happens, all you have to do is come and ask and I'll help as best I can. That's what we should be doing, sharing our knowledge and passing our experience along.'

I appreciated it then and still do.

We drove back from Zandvoort on the Friday afternoon after first qualifying for the Dutch Grand Prix and had a pleasant dinner in Amsterdam, after which he set off for his hotel and I set off for mine. My phone rang in the middle of the night and a voice from the *Daily Express* newsdesk said Murray Walker had been murdered and what did I know about it? I said we'd had dinner together and parted. I had no idea which hotel he was in and no idea how at that hour to reach anybody who might know. At some stage, as I remember, the story reached Murray that he had been murdered. No doubt his verbal dexterity did not desert him as he inquired into the precise details of his demise …

A strange story which must have been a hoax call to a newspaper, a news agency or even the BBC, but it troubled me that I might have been the prime suspect. I was the last one to clap eyes on him, after all.

We discussed the incident briefly the following day and it was never mentioned again.

Four races further on – Austria – I was able to give him proper copies of the pictures the *Express* photographer had taken after our interview and he was genuinely grateful. I recognise sincerity when I see it. I wish we'd been able to reproduce one in this book, but alas the picture library was undergoing a transfer of some kind and they were not available so you'll have to picture it for yourself: he's wearing shorts, he's smiling broadly and, even in a static pose, he looks comfortable on the bike.

If you cover Grand Prix races many faces become familiar – even now, after it has expanded so much, this still holds true – because you're all operating in a confined space. Murray was at ease within that space and somehow an integral part of it. He struck a wonderful balance with this: not too close to you and not too far away.

All this time I was covering much else besides motor racing and as a consequence was astonished, dining with him and Derick Allsop (then of the *Daily Mail*, now of the *Independent*), to discover that he knew virtually nothing about football, not even about Kevin Keegan who was then European Player of the Year. Yes, it was astonishing then – whereas now, an ignorance of football can almost be considered a desirable social grace. He had that twenty years before anybody else.

Perhaps because I was not confined to motorsport I saw aspects of it more clearly than I might otherwise have done. I covered three Winter and one Summer Olympics, all of Torvill and Dean, a lot of snooker; I interviewed (well or badly) the whole spectrum, from Steve Cram to a hammer thrower who, preparing for the Olympics, could only find a refuse dump in Essex to practise safely in, and the local authority had banned him even from that on the grounds of hygiene – so he had to pretend to throw the hammer in his back garden. I failed to interview Lester Piggott but did interview his daughter. I interviewed a black soccer player who was in the Republic of Ireland team, and before I could ask anything, he said there is one question you will want answering …

And there, every other weekend, was the man with the military gait striding along the pit lane and paddock.

One advantage of working for the BBC is that if they send you to far-flung places they lay on a car at the airport to pick you up when you get back. Murray travelled with a technician and, on one of those trips, I espied him stalking up and down at Heathrow in, clearly, a *mood*. I'd never seen this before.

'What happened?' I inquired.

'That so-and so, he got through baggage reclaim first and he's gone off in my car!!'

We had a very agreeable journey in on the tube …

I left the *Express* in 1990 because I wanted to write books, and that is what I have been doing ever since – the main weight of them about motorsport, and the main weight of that about the Grand Prix world. By the summer of 2002 Haynes had published twenty-five of these and gave me a delightful lunch in London to mark the occasion. If you compute the average length of each book as 60,000 words, that's a million and a half. And, true to the original fascination stemming from Le Mans in 1976, there always seems more to say, more to explore, more to try and explain.

I've also had published *The Wall* [in Berlin] and *The Women's War* about the events of 11 September 2001 – both from Sutton Publishing – because history interests me, particularly human history.

In a sense, that is what I have been doing with books like this one on Murray Walker too. I hope my affection and gratitude are evident but I don't want to leave it there.

I know that 1982 is fully twenty years away now but there is something I've been wanting to say ever since then. That night in Amsterdam and the hoax call – whose details remain completely obscure and surely always will.

Murray, it wasn't me.

ACKNOWLEDGEMENTS

In putting this tribute together I'm grateful to the ITV team: Martin Brundle (and his PA Margaret Cole), Jim Rosenthal, James Allen, Louise Goodman, Tony Jardine of Jardine PR, Keith Mackenzie, Debbie Austin, production co-ordinator, and press officer Paul Tyrrell. Matt Bishop, editor of *F1 Racing*, lent unused extracts from a lengthy interview and these were gratefully received. Thanks to Simon Taylor, Roger Moody (formerly BBC, now SKY), Mark Wilkin (formerly BBC, now Octagon), Mark Blundell, Julian Bailey, Jonathan Palmer of Palmer Sport; Barrie Gill, Andy Marriott and Linda Pattisson of CSS; Stuart Sykes, Gerald Donaldson, Eoin Young, Nigel Roebuck, Eddie Stephens of the D'Arcy advertising agency, Sir Stirling Moss, Raymond Baxter, Andrew Embleton, Colin Wilson, communications manager of the Motor Sport Association, Debbie Wall of Orange, Ann Bradshaw and Lynden Swainston.

Julian Kirk gave the book another dimension with his affectionate cartoons (originally in colour). Mick Woollett and Nick Nicholls scoured their archives for early pictures and I thank them, also the agencies Sporting Pictures UK Ltd (especially Sue Evans for her lightning reflexes), Formula One Pictures and LAT. Text photographs are credited as follows: page 6 LAT; page 26 Nick Nicholls; page 80 LAT; page 100 Sporting Pictures UK; page 176 ITV; page 184 LAT.

INDEX

Figures in italics refer to illustrations